NEW DIRECTIONS
FOR HIGHER EDUCATION

Number 32 • 1980

NEW DIRECTIONS
FOR HIGHER EDUCATION

A Quarterly Sourcebook
JB Lon Hefferlin, Editor-in-Chief

Number 32, 1980

Resolving Conflict in Higher Education

Jane E. McCarthy
Guest Editor

Jossey-Bass Inc., Publishers
San Francisco • Washington • London

RESOLVING CONFLICT IN HIGHER EDUCATION
New Directions for Higher Education
Volume VIII, Number 4, 1980
    Jane E. McCarthy, Guest Editor

Copyright © 1980 by Jossey-Bass Inc., Publishers
and
Jossey-Bass Limited

New Directions for Higher Education (publication number
USPS 990-880) is published quarterly by Jossey-Bass Inc., Publishers.
Subscriptions are available at the regular rate for institutions,
libraries, and agencies of $30 for one year. Individuals may
subscribe at the special professional rate of $18 for one year.
New Directions is numbered sequentially—please order extra
copies by sequential number. The volume and issue numbers
above are included for the convenience of libraries. Second-class
postage rates paid at San Francisco, California, and at
additional mailing offices.

Correspondence:
Subscriptions, single-issue orders, change of address notices,
undelivered copies, and other correspondence should be sent to
New Directions Subscriptions, Jossey-Bass Inc., Publishers,
433 California Street, San Francisco, California 94104.

Editorial correspondence should be sent to the Editor-in-Chief,
JB Lon Hefferlin, at the same address.

Library of Congress Catalogue Card Number LC 79-89400

International Standard Serial Number ISSN 0271-0560

International Standard Book Number ISBN 87589-830-0

Cover design by Willi Baum

Manufactured in the United States of America

Contents

Editor's Notes   Jane E. McCarthy   **vii**

Conflict and Mediation in   Jane E. McCarthy   **1**
the Academy

New perspectives on campus conflict suggest ways for resolving conflicts
more successfully.

Mediating the Implementation of   Jordan E. Kurland   **9**
AAUP Standards

The American Association of University Professors (AAUP) turns to
formal investigation and public censure only if its efforts at quiet and informal mediation fail.

A Mediation Service for   Patricia A. Hollander   **19**
Administrators Regarding AAUA
Standards

An organization for administrators offers a mediation service for resolving disputes concerning professional standards.

Resolving Conflict in the Upper Echelons   J. L. Zwingle   **33**

Conflict between president and governing board or within the governing board can be reduced through informal third-party intervention.

Handling Student Grievances   Janelle Shubert   **43**
in Higher Education   Joseph Folger

Appeal procedures at the University of Michigan illustrate one way institutions can protect student interests and assure due process for students.

Legal Studies and Mediation   Janet Rifkin   **49**
                                                     Peter d'Errico
                                                     Ethan Katsh

Efforts at the University of Massachusetts at Amherst illustrate how academic programs such as legal studies can form the basis for conflict resolution in the local community as well as on campus.

Taking the Initiative: Alternatives to   Linda Stamato   **55**
Government Regulation

There are ways to change higher education's reactive stance to government regulation.

Constructive Conflict in Academic Bargaining   Robert Birnbaum   69

Insights from the behavioral sciences suggest improvements in the academic bargaining process.

The Development of the Neutral Function in Labor Relations   James P. Begin   81

The acceptance of mediation and arbitration in labor disputes has evolved gradually during the history of the United States.

Further Resources   Jane E. McCarthy   91

A list of pertinent sources for further reference are given.

Index   93

Editor's Notes

Given the virtually universal recognition of the perplexing problems facing higher education, it seems extraordinary that so little attention is being devoted to developing new approaches to resolving the disputes that inevitably result when competing constituencies make legitimate demands for declining resources. The need for new approaches is dramatically illustrated by Brown University's recent out-of-court settlement of a sex-discrimination suit. The four faculty plaintiffs received a total of $48,000, but the university spent nearly $1.1 million defending itself against the suit and was ordered to pay $252,600 in lawyers' fees on behalf of the plaintiffs. No serious observer of higher education can challenge the need to create alternatives to such litigation that will provide timely and equitable solutions to disputes in higher education — solutions developed voluntarily by the parties involved without straining their resources, whether time, energy, or money. To this end, this volume of *New Directions for Higher Education* is directed to exploring current conflicts in higher education and suggesting a range of non-litigatory approaches for resolving these conflicts.

Most of the articles in this issue describe successful procedures now being used to resolve disputes without recourse to the judicial system. In "Conflict and Mediation in the Academy" I describe the work of the national Center for Mediation in Higher Education, devoted to testing the effectiveness of mediation in a wide range of disputes, including disputes on campus and disputes involving federal and state agencies. The center, in designing new procedures for resolving conflicts, seeks to strengthen collegiality by promoting approaches emphasizing shared authority and responsibility for the educational enterprise.

Next, Jordan Kurland describes the AAUP experience in negotiating settlements in disputes between faculty members and institutions over issues involving academic freedom. Then Patricia Hollander discusses the AAUA mediation service that is available to administrators in situations where there are alleged violations of the AAUA Professional Standards. And J. L. Zwingle offers suggestions from his many years of experience in assisting institutions to resolve disputes that arise within boards of trustees and between boards and presidents — disputes all too familiar to anyone who has served on governing boards or in the presidency.

Janelle Shubert and Joseph Folger of the University of Michigan next show how institutions can resolve student grievances before they burgeon into controversy or litigation, using as their example the grievance procedures of the University's Rackham School of Graduate Studies.

Then Peter d'Errico, Janet Rifkin, and Ethan Katsh discuss the Legal Studies Program at the University of Massachusetts at Amherst and the manner in which the Program's academic work in conflict resolution theory and practice has led to the design of a campus-based dispute resolution center for the University. This center will be the first dispute resolution center in the country that is organized to handle a wide variety of on-campus disputes.

Requirements for improved institutional accountability and access are at the heart of many of the seemingly intractable conflicts facing educators today. Federal antidiscrimination initiatives, in the form of government regulations on behalf of minorities, the aged and the handicapped, place costly and time-consuming reporting requirements on administrators. Linda Stamato discusses the variety of regulatory approaches being pursued by government agencies and makes a convincing case for educators to take the initiative in self-regulation.

Traditional collective bargaining procedures have served to channel conflict between faculty and administration in higher education, but they have done little to ameliorate it. Thus Robert Birnbaum offers suggestions by which unionized institutions can better use bargaining as a means of conflict resolution.

Before my suggestions about further reading, to provide an historical context for the emergence of third party neutrals, James Begin outlines the development of mediation within the framework of labor/management relations, and suggests that this experience is particularly relevant to higher education today.

This volume of *New Directions* is designed to spark discussion about alternative nonadversarial approaches to resolving disputes and to encourage initiatives in self-regulation that are compatible with the spirit of collegiality. In order to incorporate nonadversarial procedures into the decision-making process, fundamental organizational change is required; management structures will need to be altered to accommodate collaborative and consensual approaches. While institutional change occurs slowly, there is a growing interest in examining alternatives to the adversarial relationship. The procedures now being developed can be expected to receive increasing attention during the difficult years ahead for higher education.

Jane E. McCarthy
Guest Editor

Jane E. McCarthy is director of the Center for Mediation in Higher Education at the American Arbitration Association in New York. Before creating the Center in 1978, she pioneered the use of mediation procedures in environmental disputes, serving as a mediator in disputes in Washington, Rhode Island, and Maine.

New perspectives on campus conflict suggest ways for resolving conflicts more successfully.

Conflict and Mediation in the Academy

Jane E. McCarthy

Conflict is present on every college and university campus in America. Whether between or among students, faculty, administrators, boards of trustees, or state and federal agencies, conflicts are an inevitable fact of academic life.

Most educators would, no doubt, accept these propositions. However, many educators are reluctant to acknowledge the presence of specific conflicts involving them on their own campuses. Their reluctance to recognize these situations often results from their attitudes toward conflict—for example, their misperception that conflict necessarily threatens professional and collegial relationships and leads to the disruption of campus life, or their presumption that the presence of conflict suggests deficiencies in their own behavior or inadequacies in the management of the institution. This defensive reaction to conflict fails to take into account the fundamental and necessary role conflict plays in preserving existing institutional arrangements and, when managed productively, in encouraging individual and institutional adjustments to newly emerging forces and changing circumstances. What is worse, the failure to acknowledge the existence of conflict and the related hope that time or events will resolve dispute situations often exacerbates hostility and leads to destructive confrontation that could be avoided if the conflict were recognized, the issues examined, and the differences managed in a way that encourages cooperative problem-solving.

Common Areas of Conflict

To examine the range of disputes that involve higher education and to test the validity of using third party neutrals in resolving these conflicts, the Center for Mediation in Higher Education was initiated in 1978. The Center staff has reviewed a wide variety of disputes, including both those involving only campus participants and those involving the institution with outside groups.

On-campus disputes center on such issues as participation in governance, decision-making authority, internal resource allocation, changes in academic programs, and discrimination against minorities and women. These conflicts arise between and among the faculty, administration, boards of trustees, and students. Many occur because procedures for resolving disputes are perceived either as unavailable or as unsatisfactory for achieving equity.

An area of growing potential for conflict is that of planning for financial retrenchment and declining student enrollments, in light of legislative reluctance to increase state appropriations for public institutions of higher education and the need of private institutions to raise tuition and fee schedules while remaining financially competitive. Examples of financially related disputes include proposed faculty cutbacks, increased teaching loads, reassignment of tenured faculty, and the merger or elimination of academic departments, divisions, or schools.

Off-campus, jurisdictional disputes have arisen between institutions as the threat of declining full-time enrollments has fueled intense competition for part-time students and rival institutions have offered competing programs to attract these students. Federal initiatives on behalf of minorities, women, the aged, and the handicapped have engendered litigation over compliance with regulations and negotiation over costly and time-consuming reporting requirements. And, more important from the point of view of potential conflict, college and university boards of trustees and administrators must seek to accommodate opposing pressures from both traditional and new constituencies outside the academy, including demands for improved institutional accountability from coordinating boards, legislatures, and accrediting agencies, and expectations of increased access and services for poorly prepared students by community groups and agencies.

Most institutions, on a regular and sustaining basis, manage to resolve successfully the myriad disputes that arise within the academic community and between the institution and other groups. A number have established effective problem-solving mechanisms, including well-publicized grievance procedures and offices of ombudsman. But the growing pressures and demands on colleges and universities suggest that further procedures be developed and accepted to assist them on those infrequent occasions when the level of confrontation and hostility threatens to undermine normally effective existing mechanisms. Despite the fact that educators may be reluctant to recognize that the academy is occasionally susceptible to outbursts of irrational behavior, it is important for the stability of the institution that procedures be available to cope with unusual and potentially damaging conflict. Mediation is one such procedure. Not a substitute for regular problem-solving processes, it is a method of third-party assistance in resolving conflict within a framework of accommodation rather than litigation.

The Mediation Process

Traditionally, mediation has been closely associated with collective bargaining in the labor-management negotiation process. Thus there has been a tendency to confuse it with arbitration, which is also a commonly used procedure in labor-management disputes. It is important to distinguish between these two very different approaches to conflict resolution.

The sole common denominator of mediation and arbitration is the use, in both processes, of an uninvolved and neutral third party. But the role of this third party and the approach to achieving a resolution to the dispute are vastly different in the two processes. *Arbitration* is a quasi-judicial process in which the arbitrator listens to testimony and renders a decision based on this testimony. In arbitration proceedings, the parties agree in advance to accept the decision rendered by the arbitrator. In contrast, *mediation* is a collaborative process in which the parties to a dispute enter into a cooperative problem-solving venture to produce a mutually satisfactory solution, and in which they are assisted in developing their own solutions by a mediator who is not empowered to make a determination on the merits of their positions. The aim of mediation is to accommodate the important interests of the groups represented in the dispute and to produce an agreement that is acceptable to all parties. The successful resolution of the dispute is achieved when the parties explicitly agree to accept a negotiated solution that they themselves have designed.

Essential components of the mediation process include a voluntary commitment to participate and an understanding that settlement is reached only when all participants concur. But the mediator performs several important tasks which the parties usually are unable to accomplish by themselves. The mediator is responsible for ensuring that all relevant interest groups are represented in the negotiating sessions. The mediator helps the parties to communicate with each other, assisting them in ranking priority of clarifying the issues and in correcting misunderstandings. The mediator initiates and maintains an orderly negotiating process, arranges meeting places, assists in the development of an agenda. And the mediator helps to maintain the momentum of negotiations, frequently by setting deadlines to encourage movement toward settlement and constraining the tendency to procrastinate.

As a strategy for settlement, the mediator may explore the acceptability of positions that have not been presented formally by the parties. As lines of agreement emerge, the mediator assists the parties to formulate the agreement. The parties determine the form the agreement will take; it can be new guidelines, a policy statement, a memorandum of understanding or, more informally, a verbal commitment. The mediator is responsible for ensuring that the agreement is practical, in the sense that it is realistic to expect provisions in the agreement to be capable of implementation. When cooperation from outside groups is required, the mediator makes these contacts to obtain assurances that the necessary outside assistance is available.

The mediator assists the parties in working toward an agreement but cannot impose a solution on them. The mediator is selected by the parties and serves at their pleasure. It is essential to the mediator's effectiveness that he or she develop a high level of credibility and personal trust with the parties and be viewed by them as fair and impartial.

Potential for Mediation

Formidable obstacles exist to achieving acceptance for mediation in higher education, but elements within academic culture should encourage educators to use the process as an aid to dispute settlement. Chief among these is the tradition of collegiality. Many educators are concerned by the prospect that the education community's commitment to collegial governance and decision making will be threatened as institutions are forced to choose between conflicting constituencies as competition for scarce resources escalates. Mediation can foster collegiality by encouraging disputants to identify common interests and work supportively to achieve mutually acceptable solutions.

During the last year, the Center for Mediation in Higher Education has examined a number of disputes where the assistance of a mediator could have been useful in facilitating communications between the parties, discerning potential areas of agreement, encouraging the parties to work constructively to resolve their differences in a timely manner, and avoiding prolonged and costly litigation. For instance, an expensive lawsuit involving the ownership of manuscripts held by the esteemed literary journal, the *Partisan Review,* could have been avoided if the parties had agreed at the outset to seek a voluntary negotiated settlement. Instead, legal action pitted two prestigious academic institutions— Rutgers and Boston University—against each other. Outside counsel was engaged, costly and time-consuming depositions were taken, and a suit initiated. In the end, the suit was concluded with a negotiated settlement. The costs for pursuing legal action and the unwanted associated publicity might have been avoided if the parties had agreed to seek a mediated solution: The assessed value of the manuscripts was probably not substantially greater than the combined costs associated with the battle, and the victory hardly seems to have been worth the effort.

Another instance was the well-publicized case involving Wilson College in Pennsylvania, in which a judge overruled the decision of the board of trustees to close the college. Many educators view such judicial intervention into the decision-making authority of an academic institution with concern, but in order to avoid substituting the judgment of courts for that of institutional officials, viable alternatives to resolving disputes must be available. In this situation, legal action could also have been avoided, since its outcome was an agreement in the form of a consent decree signed by the litigants in which the majority of trustees agreed to resign so they could be replaced by board members favoring the continued operation of the college.

Among jurisdictional disputes involving state boards of higher education that could have been resolved more easily through mediation was one between a newly constituted state board and a regional accrediting commission over visits to public institutions in the state. The board, in exercising its review authority, proposed to initiate visits paralleling, in many respects, those of the regional commission. Eventually the board and the commission worked out an agreement to share the self-study documents prepared by public institutions, include board representatives on the accreditation teams, and share the reports prepared by the teams after their site visits, but a mediator could have assisted the board and commission and perhaps have reduced the length of time it took them to develop this solution.

In another state, the association of private colleges opposed the guidelines for the review of academic programs at private institutions that were proposed by the state board of higher education. The colleges perceived the review process as a threat to their autonomy, but rather than simply challenging the process before the board or, if necessary, in the legislature or in the courts, the association could have selected from among a variety of available alternatives. Among them, the private colleges could have agreed to submit their own review procedures voluntarily to the board for its possible acceptance. In the process of reaching a compromise between the association and the board, a neutral could have assisted them in interpreting positions, clarifying intentions, and encouraging negotiations.

Barriers to Mediation

A mediator can often channel resentment and anger into more constructive approaches, absorbing antagonism between parties and minimizing destructive confrontation that can adversely affect relationships between the parties. Several distinctive features of higher education, however, tend to work against the introduction of mediation. For example, members of the academic community are frequently reluctant to discuss dispute situations in which they are involved, for fear of jeopardizing their careers, alienating friends and colleagues, or receiving unfavorable publicity for advocating unpopular positions. Thus, the absence of direct confrontation makes it difficult to identify dispute situations.

In addition, institutional or organizational constraints tend to hide or minimize the presence of conflict. Governance at many institutions is ill defined and diffused, characterized by overlapping jurisdictions and indefinite leadership roles. This ambiguous decision-making structure tends to conceal conflict, clouding the interests and needs of the parties.

Further difficulties arise from the widely held perception that engaging the services of a mediator from outside the institution is a reflection on the quality and effectiveness of institutional administrators, faculty leaders, or trustees—the belief that an institution should be able to resolve problems internally without requesting outside assistance. Under these circumstances, considerable effort must be expended to develop an understanding of the role of a mediator and to assure participants that their interests will be fully represented without endangering their professional progress, collegial relationships, reputations, or self-worth.

Elements of Effective Mediation

For mediators to be effective in disputes in higher education, they must be attuned to the unique characteristics of the academic community. They must have a thorough understanding of the unique organizational structure and management of the institution where the dispute occurs, including the role of trustees, faculty, administrators, and student groups, and an understanding of the outside forces that limit the authority of these groups, such as state legislators, boards of higher education, and federal enforcement agencies. They must not only develop a high level of personal trust among the parties but also be sure the parties understand the nature of the mediation process. Because participants in the process are keenly sensitive about maintaining their professional and personal standing, it is incumbent on the mediator to exercise extreme care in investigating, assessing, and participating in the dispute resolution process.

A distinguishing feature of mediation in higher education is its informality and lack of specificity in the negotiating process. As noted above, institutional officials can be extremely sensitive about the use of third-party neutrals, feeling that the use of an outsider is a sign of weakness and an inability to manage effectively. This suggests that effective academic mediation requires a minimum of publicity and a maximum effort by mediators in playing down their role in achieving settlements. For example, when the parties are reluctant to acknowledge the formal assistance of a mediator, the neutral can refrain from using the label "mediator" and be viewed instead as an informal advisor.

The need to minimize the active role of an outsider is an additional factor that makes it difficult for the parties to put any agreement in writing. Here the mediation process in nonlabor disputes in higher education differs in some respects from the accustomed application of the process in other fields, where the goal is to achieve a negotiated settlement that takes the form of a written document, drafted cooperatively by the parties and describing the understanding that has been reached. This document of agreement is the "product" of a successful mediation effort. In higher education, the "product" frequently takes other forms, such as the adaptation of existing rules, guidelines, or policies. In dispute situations the Center has examined such agreements have taken several forms: a policy statement issued by the administration, a state board statement of cooperation with accrediting commission evaluation teams, or a section of a state master plan describing the reporting requirements for private colleges. In disputes involving minority students, the "product" could be an oral agreement that new courses will be offered in minority studies or the formation of a student-administration committee to develop strategies for improving race relations on campus. Hence the mediator should not expect, as a matter of course, to produce a free-standing document signed by the parties.

Since the mediator's role in academic disputes varies widely from case to case, mediators must take their cues from the parties, reacting to their needs and sensitivities. For instance, a mediator may work with the parties separately for many weeks before scheduling a first joint session where all parties will be represented. During these weeks, the mediator will seek to identify the substantive issues, interpret the positions of the parties to each other, and clarify misunderstandings concerning each other's needs and objectives. If the parties were brought together prematurely, they might be unable to approach constructively the problems to be resolved and concentrate instead on the unfortunate incidents that precipitated the crisis leading to the impasse. An effective mediator will absorb the emotional heat generated by the opposing parties, allowing them to move toward practical approaches to resolving outstanding disagreements.

Role of the Center for Mediation in Higher Education

The Center's involvement in dispute situations comes about as a result of one or more of the parties contacting the Center. When a request is received, the Center's director assesses the situation on a preliminary basis to determine the prospects for mediation. If appropriate, a site visit is arranged to discuss the dispute with the parties involved, but this step is taken only when all the parties have agreed to discuss the dispute with an uninvolved third party. In this phase, the parties need not have made a decision regarding their acceptance of either the mediation process or a specific mediator.

If the parties agree to initiate negotiations with the assistance of a mediator, a member of the Center meets with them and suggests names of persons who would be appropriate mediators. In some instances a mediation team, rather than an individual mediator, seems to serve the best interests of the parties. Usually, mediators are members of the higher education community familiar with the general issues in dispute. When the parties have agreed on the selection of a mediator or mediators, the Center contacts them and the process will be initiated.

The costs associated with mediation are shared between the Center and the institution. The Center usually underwrites the expenses involved in the premediation assessment stage; while the institution assumes the costs associated with the actual mediation process.

In helping institutions use nonadversarial procedures for settling disputes, the Center has increasingly recognized the need of institutions to develop and refine their regularized on-campus due process procedures. Responsive and and timely grievance and compliant procedures are needed not only for the protection of faculty, but also for administrators, professional and support staff, and students. The Center has initiated a two-part project to assist institutions in developing grievance mechanisms incorporating a mediation component. First, consultants from the Center who have experience in designing these procedures are available to assist grievance procedure review committees to develop accessible, nonadversarial procedures to serve the variety of interests that comprise the higher education community. Second, the Center is designing a model grievance procedure for use by institutions in drafting their own procedures. This model contains a variety of options, depending on whether the institution drafts procedures to cover all campus groups or only one constituent group, such as the faculty, and depending on the kinds of grievances to be included, such as salary, promotion, tenure, discrimination, or complaints of all kinds. It describes alternate steps in nonadversarial procedures, depending on whether the institution elects to include mediation, fact finding, or a final arbitration step. And it illustrates a variety of options regarding representation on a grievance committee, hearings, time limits, forms of agreement, levels of appeals, and reporting requirements.

Conclusion

The constituency for mediation is expected to build gradually as the academic community and government officials develop an understanding of the process and its potential application in higher education. Nonadversarial approaches to conflict resolution should receive increasing attention from educators who face ever expanding government regulations, stable budgets, and diminished spending power. Among these approaches, mediation, with its emphasis on accommodation and cooperative problem solving, can reinforce the education community's long-standing commitment to reasoned discourse and collegiality, and the Center for Mediation in Higher Education stands ready to aid this process.

Jane E. McCarthy is director of the Center for Mediation in Higher Education at the American Arbitration Association in New York.

The American Association of University Professors turns to formal investigation and public censure only if its efforts at quiet and informal mediation fail.

Mediating the Implementation of AAUP Standards

Jordan E. Kurland

The American Association of University Professors, since its inception in 1915, has been the leading agency in higher education in developing the principles and standards governing the relationships of academic life. Often in conjunction with other national organizations, AAUP has issued such landmark documents as the 1940 *Statement of Principles on Academic Freedom and Tenure* (with the Association of American Colleges) and the 1966 *Statement on Government of Colleges and Universities* (with the American Council on Education and the Association of Governing Boards of Universities and Colleges joining in its formulation). Other AAUP statements, to name a few, deal with dismissal proceedings, renewal of appointments, professional ethics, political activity, discrimination, recruitment, resignation, and retirement. Currently thirty-six of these statements are compiled for ready reference in AAUP's *Policy Documents and Reports.*

The Association, however, also from its very inception, has assumed responsibility not only for promulgating principles and standards but for implementing them in specific situations. AAUP's first president, John Dewey, set the tone as follows in his 1915 Presidential Address (pp. 11–12): "Some have expressed to me fear lest attention to individual grievances might crowd out attention to those general and 'constructive' matters which are the Association's reason for existence . . . . The investigations of particular cases were literally thrust upon us. To have failed to meet the demands would have been cowardly;

it would have tended to destroy all confidence in the Association as anything more than a talking body. The question primarily involved was . . . whether the Association was to have legs and arms and be a working body."

To an extent which would have astonished and delighted Professor Dewey, the Association has indeed emerged as a working body. Its legs and arms scramble to deal with over 2,000 inquiries each year on particular problems relating to AAUP standards. Some of these inquiries are dealt with by a single response, but about half of them lead to the opening of a file on a formal complaint by one or more faculty members against an institution's administrative officers or sometimes against other members of the faculty. These complaints, numbering approximately 1,100 annually in recent years and dealing with the academic status of one or more individuals, are processed by members of the Association's professional staff, located in AAUP's national office in Washington, D.C., and in regional offices in New York, San Francisco, and the mid-West. The staff is guided in its work by various Association policy-making bodies, especially its Committee A on Academic Freedom and Tenure, and it can often call upon the officers of AAUP's 1,300 local chapters or the 46 state-wide AAUP affiliates or other capable volunteers for assistance.

Scope of AAUP Concerns

The chief interest of the Association in processing these complaints is to employ its good offices in bringing them to a resolution which comports with AAUP standards and, whenever possible, is satisfactory to the parties directly concerned. Before discussing AAUP's mediative role, it should be noted that many complaints are not opportune for or susceptible to AAUP mediation, in which instances AAUP's response can take other forms. Often there are appropriate informal or formal procedures within the institution which can and should be used, in which event AAUP will provide procedural advice but avoid direct involvement. Where a collective bargaining agreement with the faculty is in force, a dispute may go to outside arbitration, and the Association may address itself to the scope of what is to be arbitrated and to the criteria to be followed. Litigation may already have been entered or may be the only feasible course to pursue. The Association often enters a legal case, usually at the appellate level, as a friend of the court, when the decision is likely to have an impact on basic AAUP standards. In addition, the Association has an Academic Freedom Fund and a Legal Defense Fund to aid in the litigation of issues of AAUP concern. In like manner, the Association may provide assistance in a complaint which is before a governmental agency. When what is known about a complaint suggests violation of principles of academic freedom and tenure, and the institution's administration simply refuses to discuss the matter, the Association may proceed quite promptly to a formal investigation; the procedures for investigating and imposing censure will be noted later. Whenever it can, however, the Association's staff seeks to mediate an appropriate resolution.

Consistent with its aim of upholding its principles and standards rather than representing the interests of individuals, the Association does not require faculty members to join the organization in order to process their complaints. Its view has always been that unrectified departures from sound academic standards do injury to the entire academic profession, AAUP members and nonmembers alike. AAUP will receive a complaint from any teacher, research scholar, librarian, or counselor who has faculty status at an approved college or university. While most often it is the complaining faculty member who initially approaches the Association's staff about the problem, it is not at all unusual for the first word to come from the local AAUP chapter, the department chairman, a faculty committee dealing with the matter, or a member of the administration. Administrators frequently consult with the Association on how to deal with a situation involving a faculty member, and on many occasions the staff's advice has led to a solution and thus kept a complaint from arising. When someone other than the prospective complainant initiates the inquiry to the Association, the staff will ask that the individual directly concerned be invited to write or call. If the matter seems sufficiently serious or urgent, the staff will not stand on ceremony but will itself get in touch with the individual and make its availability known.

Staff Assistance to Complaints

Apprised of a complaint, the Association's staff comes to a prompt preliminary assessment of its urgency and of its potential gravity under Association standards. The complaint of the faculty member who reports that he has just been dismissed and has been ordered off the premises by the end of that afternoon obviously calls for a different order of response from that of the faculty member who complains that the institution is contributing insufficiently to his pension which will become effective upon his retirement thirty years hence. The faculty member may present a complaint that is legitimate enough but raises no issues under Association standards (for example, that the institution overemphasizes football or admits ill-prepared students), in which case the staff can do little more than advise as to sources within the institution for dealing with these concerns. The staff must on occasion attempt to explain to a faculty member that the Association, while ever vigilant in its defense of academic freedom, cannot assert that academic freedom is on the line in a dispute over the allocation of a parking space. If the problem appears to be both urgent and severe as regards Association standards, the staff will move as quickly as it can to establish contact with the institution's administration in an endeavor to ameliorate the situation, or at least stop it from worsening, while at the same time soliciting additional information from the faculty member and others to enable it to analyze the dimensions of the problem and the nature of the Association's concerns.

Should a complaint appear to the staff to be invalid or superficial or trivial, it is the staff member's responsibility to advise the complaint that the Association will probably not pursue it and that it might be in his or her best interests not to pursue it. Should a complaint, in the staff's judgment, be legitimate yet only "five miles over the speed limit," it is incumbent upon the staff to review carefully and patiently with the faculty member whether his or her energies, as well as any expression of Association interest, might better be invested in the instant question or reserved for another day.

When the facts presented by the complainant and others do seem to support an allegation that Association standards, or the institution's own regulations, have been violated, the staff must then decide upon the approach which best serves the situation at hand. The staff, more often than not, is equipped to assess the situation through its experience with other cases, at that institution and elsewhere, and through the Association's knowledge of the institution's stated policies and actual practices, of its previous dealings with the institution's administration, and of the strength and capability of the institution's instruments of faculty government and AAUP chapter as well as individual AAUP members at the institution and at institutions nearby. While staff members are certainly aware that they can recommend formal investigation of a case which poses a serious infraction of Association standards, their interest in the first instance is in mediation, in negotiating a resolution that will preclude the need for formal and public action.

When the Association's staff member who is handling a faculty member's complaint is in insufficient command of the facts to advance a particular position, he or she will, with the faculty member's consent, contact the institution's administration, usually the chief administrative officer. This approach may be indirect, through the AAUP chapter or through a particular AAUP representative in the area. The contact may be through letter, telegram, telephone (used increasingly in this day and age), or personal visit. The available information on the complaint will be presented, together with the issues it appears to raise under Association standards. The comments of the administration will be solicited. Assuming the accuracy of the Association's information, one or more recommended resolutions will be proposed or discussion will be invited. This presentation, and discussions which ensue, can be highly formal or informal depending upon the circumstances.

The response received from the administration may, if the faculty member cannot effectively rebut it, demolish the validity of the faculty member's complaint, in which case the staff will "close the file." Alternately, the administration's response may provide little or nothing which refutes the faculty member's contentions, leading the staff to reassert its recommendation for a resolution, with a formal investigation in prospect if a resolution is not forthcoming. As often as not, the respective positions of the faculty member and the administration present a mixed picture, leading the Association's staff to urge the wisdom of a mutually acceptable accommodation. In approximately half of the cases in which the staff presents issues under the Association's standards to an institutional administration and urges an acceptable resolution, that resolution is achieved through the staff's mediative efforts.

Investigation of Unresolved Cases

Those serious cases which remain unresolved are carefully reviewed by a staff committee responsible for recommending to the Association's General Secretary that a formal investigation be authorized. Under Association procedures, the General Secretary, AAUP's chief administrative officer, has the sole responsibility for authorizing an investigation. The General Secretary makes this decision upon determination of an apparent major yet unresolved violation of the 1940 *Statement of Principles on Academic Freedom and Tenure* and derivative principles and standards. The case is submitted to an ad hoc committee of qualified active members of the Association who have had no previous involvement in the matter. Between a half dozen and a dozen such cases reach this stage and are investigated annually, according to the figures of the last few years.

An ad hoc investigation committee, after examining the documentation available to the Association, visits the college or university on preannounced dates and meets with the parties directly concerned as well as with others who wish to speak not only to the case at hand but to other matters bearing upon Association principles and standards. The investigating committee is charged with preparing a report for submission to the Association's Committee A on Academic Freedom and Tenure. Just as the General Secretary is the sole official who can authorize an investigation, Committee A, which deals with a particular case for the first time when it receives an investigating committee's report, is the sole body within the Association which can authorize the report's publication.

Some cases authorized for investigation attain satisfactory resolution before an investigation results in a published report (the staff is unceasingly alert to opportunities for mediation), and occasionally a case is resolved soon after a report appears. Immediately before the Association's Annual Meeting each spring, Committee A reviews the reports published during the preceding year together with any subsequent developments relating to these reports. The Committee formulates recommendations to the Annual Meeting which may call for censure, the Association's strongest sanction, of an institutional administration found to be in violation of accepted academic standards. As the General Secretary is alone empowered to authorize an investigation and Committee A is alone empowered to publish a report and thus bring the case before the academic community, only the Annual Meeting is empowered to impose a censure (and subsequently to remove it). Presently there are forty-six institutions on the Association's list of Censured Administrations.

The censure list is not a blacklist. The Association will not and probably could not compel its members, let alone its nonmembers, to refuse to accept positions at censured institutions. The aim is to keep the censure in the public eye while being alert to developments that will permit a recommendation to a subsequent Annual Meeting for removal. The list is published in each issue of the Association's journal, *Academe: Bulletin of the AAUP,* which appears eight times per year, and once a year there is a published record of new developments relating to each censure. Faculty members are advised, before accepting appointments at the institutions on the list, to consult with the Association's staff and with prospective departmental colleagues and then to make their own decision. The list is published periodically in Canada, by the Canadian Association of University Teachers, and it appears in Great Britain as well. Many of the learned societies and professional organizations that have endorsed the 1940 *Statement of Principles* also publish the list regularly and note the existence of the censure when they carry an announcement of an academic vacancy at the affected institution. Phi Beta Kappa, an endorser of the 1940 *Statement,* has declined to approve new chapters at censured institutions and has urged existing chapters to seek improved conditions.

The Association has specific procedures for the removal of censure as well as for its imposition. Considerations include the official adoption of institutional regulations in essential conformity with Association standards, redress to the faculty member whose case was the basis of the censure, and evidence of a satisfactory current climate for academic freedom and tenure. Censure has been removed as soon as one year after it was imposed. The current forty-six censured institutions have been on the Association's list from one to eighteen years. The first investigation by the Association occurred in 1915, and the first censure was imposed in 1933. The longest censure on record lasted twenty years. (That same institution was censured again fourteen years later, and the second censure lasted only two years.) But the Association's postcensure negotiations have in all cases, sooner or later, met with success. Each and every censured institution, if not through the same erring administration then through a successor administration, has eventually cooperated with the Association in reforming the policies and practices which were the subject of the Association's initial concern.

Examples of Informal Mediation

While the Association can point with pride to what it has accomplished through investigation and censure, these publicly visible endeavors are, however, in a sense the Association's failures. As was emphasized earlier, the Association's chief interest is in securing an acceptable resolution through its informal mediative techniques and thus avoiding the need for formal and protracted action. Sometimes a resolution is so long in coming that even informal mediation is protracted, but the staff keeps at it. One file, on the complaint of a professor who claimed she was unfairly kept at a low salary, remained open until her retirement while intermittent approaches to the administration brought no adjustment. Some nine years later, a new administration took office, and the staff tried again. The result was a retroactive increase in the retired professor's pension, amounting to nearly $20,000. Most of the time, however, justice comes much quicker. The shortest open complaint within memory involved an instructor who called to report that he was unexpectedly being reduced to part-time status. The staff member who took the call immediately telephoned the instructor's dean, who promised to rectify the matter without delay. The dean called the instructor, who in turn called the staff member back to report happily that he had been assured of continuance in his full-time position. The time that elapsed between the instructor's first call, presenting the complaint, and his second call, bringing notification of its resolution, was exactly fifteen minutes.

Association staff members write brief accounts of successfully mediated complaints. The text of a few such accounts, selected from among several dozen files which were closed in recent months following satisfactory mediation, will provide some indication of the nature of the problems and of the Association's role.

1. A faculty member at a small professional school in the Northeast was dismissed for cause prior to the expiration of his term of appointment. The Association's staff, once it reviewed the record of the proceeding, stated to the administration that significant protections of academic due process had not been provided. The staff also questioned whether cause was of the magnitude to justify dismissal had been demonstrated. The administration acknowledged that the procedures which had been used, adopted ad hoc for the particular case, were not satisfactory. At a subsequent meeting of the governing board, regular dismissal proceedings, formulated with staff assistance and based on the 1958 *Statement on Procedural Standards,* were approved as institutional policy. With regard to the case in question, the administration, which had continued the faculty member's salary during the remaining three months of the term of his original appointment, offered to pay him an additional three months as settlement of the case.

2. At an independent college in the Middle Atlantic states, a faculty member accepted a probationary appointment with the written understanding that he would have six years in which to qualify for tenure. Two years later, when his qualifications were reviewed in connection with reappointment for a second three-year term, the administration noted that he had three years of prior service elsewhere. Although the crediting of this previous service was mandatory under an institutional regulation, the faculty member had not been aware that the regulation applied to his case and the administration acknowledged that the earlier service had simply been overlooked at the time of initial appointment. Both parties, appreciating that the faculty member could not qualify for tenure if the decision had to be made within a year but probably would qualify if he

could serve the full six years at the college before a decision was reached, turned to the Association for assistance. A staff member informed them that the Association would not take issue with a waiver of the prior service in this case, given the written understanding at the time of initial appointment and the inadvertent failure to take the prior service into account. The staff member assisted in the formulation of an agreement, under which the parties agreed to an exception to the institutional regulation with the understanding that there would be no subsequent claim to tenure by the faculty member merely on grounds of length of service as a result of this agreement.

3. A tenured professor at a state university in the South was notified by the administration in January that because of financial considerations his program, which attracts relatively few students, had been recommended by a faculty-administration committee for discontinuance and his services would therefore be terminated at the end of the academic year. A member of the Association's staff proceeded to discuss the matter with the administration. He emphasized that whatever the merits of the recommendation to terminate the program and thus the professor's appointment, merits which would be determined through a hearing that the administration was prepared to offer, the notice of less than six months was unacceptably brief. Six days later, the staff member was informed that the president of the university, finding the financial situation not so severe as had been earlier estimated and agreeing that the notice was inadequate, rejected the recommendation to discontinue the program. The professor was informed that the notice was being rescinded and that his retention for the following academic year was assured.

4. A professor at a small private college in the Midwest, suffering from medical disability, was placed on leave of absence and then informed by the administration that his services would be terminated after another three months. The professor turned for assistance to the Association's staff, which conveyed concern to the administration over the apparent lack of academic due process preceding its action and over the inadequate notice of termination. Discussion of a mutually acceptable resolution commenced. Before the expiration of the three months, the administration extended an offer which the professor accepted. He is being continued at the college, in a largely honorary administrative position at half his current salary, for an additional four years at which time he will reach the age of retirement.

Conclusion

The American Association of University Professors emphasizes the need for sound procedural standards appropriate to an academic setting but seeks in its mediative work to call upon reason and fairness rather than make threats or stand on technicalities. A faculty member who points to an inadvertent technical violation of stated institutional procedures, but cannot show that any actual harm has resulted from the lapse, will be informed that the Association is not prepared to argue that the institution should provide redress. In a case where formal institutional and AAUP standards have not been breached, yet the faculty member has nonetheless suffered from inequitable treatment, the Association will assert that redress is warranted. During the course of negotiations, the Association's staff is perhaps more likely to stress the plight of a human being while the institution's administrators stress orderly and economical management. Still, the Association well recognizes, as it protects individual rights, that the welfare of the academic institution must also be preserved.

Writing ten years ago about the Association's mediative work, Bertram H. Davis, AAUP's General Secretary at the time, concluded (1970, p. 173): "Through a persistent vigilance — through the constant application of its principles to cases — the Association has made academic freedom a byword in higher education, and in institution after institution it has been instrumental in the adoption of policies and procedures which lend support to academic freedom. To individual faculty members it has given a resource in their hour of need, and to faculties as a whole it has steadily helped to bring the dignity of professional status."

We continue to perform this vital task for the members of our profession and for the academic community in which they serve.

References

Davis, B. H. *AAUP Bulletin,* Summer 1970, p. 173.
Dewey, J. "Presidential Address." *AAUP Bulletin,* December 1915, pp. 11–12.

Jordan E. Kurland was a professor of history at the University of North Carolina before joining the AAUP staff in 1965. He became associate general secretary in 1969 and for the last decade has directed the AAUP staff work on academic freedom and tenure cases.

An organization for administrators offers a mediation service for resolving disputes concerning professional standards.

A Mediation Service for Administrators Regarding AAUA Standards

Patricia A. Hollander

The American Association of University Administrators (AAUA), founded in 1970 by a group of administrators at the State University of New York at Buffalo, and with its national office now in Oneonta, New York, is an individual membership association of college and university administrators who are dedicated to the improvement of the profession of higher education administration. Its membership numbers some 1600 administrators in the United States and Canada with some additional members in the United Kingdom and Europe. They include presidents, vice-presidents, deans, program directors, chairpersons, librarians, registrars, admissions and placement officers, and other professional staff at all types of institutions. Academic affairs officers comprise the largest group of AAUA members, with student affairs and business officers following in numbers.

AAUA has adopted a policy of not becoming a collective bargaining agent for administrators. However, for the past eight years it has served as a mediator in disputes concerning collective bargaining or involving college and university administrators. Use of its service has increased every year, and by 1980 some seventy requests for assistance had been received. In most instances, AAUA has been contacted by individual administrators. Sometimes, however, several administrators have joined together and asked for AAUA's help as a group. Institutions at large have also sought the assistance of AAUA.

AAUA makes its mediation service available by virtue of its role of advocate of its *Professional Standards for Administrators in Higher Education,** and at present it undertakes only those cases that appear to violate some portion of the Standards. These Standards, adopted in 1975 after three years of successful experimental use by the Association, set forth concomitant responsibilities and rights for administrators. Their rationale is that "just as academic freedom is the special hallmark of institutions of higher education, so, too, is academic responsibility the correlative of such freedom . . . . The exercise of academic responsibility and academic freedom by administrators requires clearly understood (1) conditions of employment, (2) parameters of the operation of the office, (3) career considerations, and (4) personal responsibilities and rights."

AAUA views the Standards as benchmarks to be used by administrators, other individuals, and institutions in developing and interpreting policies and practices affecting administrators and in seeking amicable solutions to disputes. In a normative way, they afford a guide against which to measure professionalism. For example, they provide that an administrator has the responsibility to carry out the duties of the office as noted in the written statement of the conditions of employment or in the job description published in an official handbook of the institution. By the same token, an administrator has a right to a written statement of the conditions of employment, including, but not limited to: (1) statements on salary and fringe benefits, (2) term of office, (3) process of review, (4) date by which notification of action regarding renewal or continuance will be forthcoming, and (5) responsibilities of the position. Similarly, the Standards affirm that administrators are responsible for implementing institutional policy as set by the governing board, and that this duty brings with it the right to have adequate authority to carry out these responsibilities. Administrators have the responsibility to avoid arbitrary and capricious actions regarding subordinates, and are entitled to expect the same from their superiors, whether other administrators or the governing board. And administrators have the responsibility to respect the personal privacy of others, and in turn to have personal privacy.

When administrators, other individuals, or institutions believe that these Standards have not been complied with, they may contact AAUA's Standards and Review Committee and request its assistance. AAUA's intent in handling these requests is to seek an amicable solution to the problem through mediation. Since the requestor is usually an aggrieved administrator, AAUA's first aim is to assist the administrator in securing a remedy for the alleged injury suffered due to the violation of the Standards. This remedy often removes a cloud from

*Copies of the *AAUA Professional Standards for Administrators in Higher Education* may be obtained from Dr. Robert W. MacVittie, General Secretary, AAUA, P.O. Box 536, Oneonta, NY 13820.

the administrator's professional reputation and sometimes involves compensation for arbitrary and capricious action. AAUA's second aim is to assist the institution, when appropriate, to develop and adopt policies and procedures regarding its administrators that conform with the Standards. Accordingly, AAUA's advocacy of its Standards is a collegial, not an adversarial, activity. It uses no sanctions or blacklisting arrangements against institutions or individuals, since its role is advisory and constructive.

In this regard, AAUA views mediation as a method that should be used to solve most problems between responsible professionals. Mediation protects the parties' autonomy, in that it helps the parties themselves find a solution to their problem. No outside solution is imposed. The settlement is completely voluntary. The mediator's role is to clarify issues, make suggestions, and do all possible to strip away extraneous issues so that the parties may reach some area of common ground. Once that is done, the mediator provides as many alternative ideas for solution as possible. The emphasis is on fair play and on solutions reached inside the academy consonant with academic values and practices.

Causes of Disputes Mediated by AAUA

AAUA has been able to identify a number of major causes of disputes, whether between administrators and institutions, administrators and faculty senates or unions, administrators and faculty members, administrators and students, or administrators and various off-campus public officials, press, and individuals. Initial contact with AAUA often results from termination of an administrator by the institution. However, it is clear from an analysis of the requests for assistance processed by AAUA that such an act is merely the surface of the dispute. Underlying most terminations are an array of problems that are repeated with dismaying regularity. Prominent among these are a lack of clear written institutional policies in general and non-existent or poorly defined personnel policies for administrators in particular. Usually, some degree of mutual understanding is lacking between the administrator and his or her employer regarding basic matters such as the job description and the responsibilities and rights associated with the position. This often reflects the lack of routine practices such as periodic evaluation, clear notice of termination, appeal or review processes, and agreement regarding a letter of recommendation for the terminated individual.

AAUA studies have shown that if written statements of conditions of employment were honored as much in the observance as in the breach, significant losses in money and reputation would be saved by institutions and administrators. Even one such lawsuit per year would likely cover the annual salary of an administrator or faculty member. Most institutions have learned the hard way — regrettably, by litigation — that the traditional practice of having administrators serve entirely at the pleasure of their supervisors is an irresponsible and costly practice. It violates numerous good management practices beginning with accountability for personnel decisions. The cost of recruiting, hiring, and training new personnel is high, and written job descriptions combined with regular evaluation procedures for early decisions regarding continuance of employment are cost effective in the long run. Fewer disputes occur when employment contracts and practices are reduced to writing than when the staff is at the mercy of managers who make decisions by whim. Such decisions are likely to be challenged in court and, depending on evidence regarding the mutual agreement of the parties or the prevailing practice in the profession, they may result in awards of compensatory and even punitive damages.

Another consistent pattern in many of the termination cases involves personal incompatibility. Typically, an administrator may be dismissed as incompetent; but the facts indicate that the true reason for termination is incompatibility of administrative styles with a superior. Obviously, instances of incompetence do occur, but they seldom reach the stage of mediation.

A third source of termination involves major financial problems at an institution resulting in drastic organizational changes such as a complete administrative reorganization, a combination of two administrative units into one, or the discontinuance of a division or department. In times of financial crisis, it becomes painfully evident that plans for it have not been made in advance. Both administrators and faculty are faced with various cost-cutting schemes without forewarning or consultation in the decision-making process. For instance, a division head at one university first learned that he was about to be terminated when he read a press release issued in the president's name announcing that the division was about to be abolished because of budgetary restrictions. Having procedures in place for prior consultation when confronting financial problems most probably would have prevented the embarassment to the institution caused by unfavorable press surrounding this episode.

Governing board actions may also be the basis for requests for mediation. Interestingly enough, some problems have been found to arise simply because members of boards of trustees lack experience or have been inadequately informed about their responsibilities and procedures. One college president suddenly stopped receiving pay checks after twenty years as president. A largely new board had decided to fire him. He was ordered to turn over his keys, his office locks were changed, and his successor rummaged through his personal effects before returning them to him. A satisfactory settlement was eventually reached by mediation, but mediation could have been used earlier by the board to find a professionally acceptable method of replacing the president and avoiding the adverse publicity generated by his firing.

The appointment of a new chief administrative officer, such as a president or a chancellor, may be the occasion for "cleaning house," but a chaotic and poorly coordinated reorganization may result in severe dislocations in ongoing or newly developed departments or programs. In such cases, long-time administrators may be seen by the new executive as doing a poor job when, in fact, the problem is that the executive has not yet fully determined what job the administrators are supposed to do. At one large state institution, for example, shortly after a new president was appointed, the vice-president for student affairs learned through a press release that he was being fired, the student affairs office was to be reorganized, and his three assistants were not being retained. The new president apparently was not able to handle this reorganization in a professional manner. Mediation could have helped the parties develop procedures, even on a temporary basis, to communicate and to affect an orderly transition. Instead, mediation was brought to bear after the fact to rescue the professional reputations of the vice-president and his assistants and to assist the institution in developing better procedures to handle such situations.

The overall governance structure of an institution may be another source of problems for administrators. Components of this structure include the faculty senate, the student governing body, members of the community, the local press, collective bargaining agents, alumni, state departments or boards of education, and other groups who have a stake in the policies and operation of the institution or of its parent system. Any of these may be the source of various kinds and levels of misunderstandings. At one college with both a faculty senate and a faculty union, for example, where retrenchment became a necessity, a disagreement developed over how much notice of personnel actions should be given. The faculty union wanted six months' notice of nonrenewal for those affected so that they would have ample time to seek new employment. The administration thought two months' notice was adequate because this would permit sufficient time to prepare accurate financial projections and thereby limit the terminations to only three or four faculty members. The faculty senate refused to help make the necessary projections, which the administration thought was an abrogation of responsibility. The union convinced the administration to give six months' notice, but to err on the safe side, the administration sent termination notices to twelve faculty members, anticipating that some of these notices could be recalled later. As a result, no one was satisfied. A modus operandi finally was devised, but earlier mediation could have prevented much animosity, lack of confidence, and feelings of mistrust.

Accreditation processes, too, have given rise to problems resulting in the termination of administrators. Very often this appears to develop from the belief that an issue raised by an accreditation report can be solved by replacing an administrator, when, in fact, removing a particular administrator may have little effect on an endemic organizational problem. For instance, at a large independent university, an accreditation team found that the roles of the administrators were defined indistinctly, the decision-making process was confused, and communication within the institution's administrative structure was poor. The team also cited a specific lack of knowledge by the administration and faculty regarding the activities of the office for student affairs. Subsequently, the vice-president for student affairs was abruptly dismissed without a reason being given. With mediation, his professional reputation was salvaged through a letter of recommendation which accurately reflected the facts, and he received compensation for the arbitrary action. But mediation prior to his dismissal would have assisted the parties in limiting the subsequent tangles.

Requests for AAUA assistance also result from disagreements based on attempts by administrators to interpret and comply with federal or state regulations, such as those prohibiting discrimination toward minorities and women. Administrators having the responsibility in such areas may be caught between their supervisor's interpretation of a set of legal regulations and that of a state or federal agency. Thus at one independent college, the vice-president for business affairs had the responsibility for filing compliance forms regarding federal employment regulations, but he and the president could not agree on what steps were required for compliance. The vice-president was fired. He recovered damages in a breach of contract suit, and provision for an accurate letter of recommendation was mediated. A new president took over soon after. This incident, too, might well have been handled by mediation at a much earlier stage.

AAUA Procedures to Mediate Disputes

The mediation procedures used by AAUA's Standards and Review Committee involve a three-step process. The service is available to persons on behalf of themselves or their institutions, whether or not they are members of AAUA, although priority may be given to AAUA members. AAUA provides the service as a benefit to the profession of higher education administration, rather than to any particular individual or institution.

First Step: Inquiry. Step One of the mediation process involves an administrator or other individual submitting a written request for assistance, indicating which of the AAUA Standards is thought to have been violated. AAUA determines from this initial information whether the situation involves the Standards and accepts only those cases that do relate to their violation. The requester may ask that initial assistance be confidential. This option is available so that the requester may consult privately with an AAUA representative about the details of the situation, consider various alternatives, and have the opportunity to resolve the matter without overt intervention from AAUA. A number of situations have been handled in this fashion at the request of the inquirer. AAUA insists that requesters exhaust internal remedies before it will undertake their case, and explains that once Step One has been taken, AAUA will continue the case to the end, even though the individual requests that it be withdrawn, if AAUA feels such continuance benefits the profession.

AAUA's mediation process does not require the voluntary consent of all parties to the dispute, as do some mediation methods. Once AAUA is asked to look into a situation, it enters principally on behalf of the profession. If one of the parties chooses not to cooperate, AAUA will do the best it can to gather all the facts before taking action, but it will not be deterred from doing its best to resolve the problem.

Second Step: Visitation. Step Two involves a mediation team visit to the site for a preliminary inquiry and review. At this stage, the chairperson of AAUA's Standards and Review Committee informs the "other party" to the dispute, such as the president or chairman of the governing board, that a request for assistance has been filed and that a team will be investigating the case. It has been AAUA's experience that once this other party understands that AAUA is serving as an advocate of its Standards rather than of the individual complainant, confidence and cooperation in the process develop.

AAUA's Standards and Review Committee names a team of mediators and designates one of the team members as its chairperson. That person's responsibility is to make arrangements for the team to interview the requester and his or her witnesses, and to collect facts or add to the information available for a factual summary of the case. If it is inconvenient or awkward for the team to meet with the requester and the witnesses on campus, an off-campus site such as a motel room can be used. Normally, the team chairperson also contacts the appropriate institutional representative to set up a meeting to hear the other party's view and secure pertinent facts from that perspective. When an administrator who has been or is about to be terminated from an institution has requested AAUA mediation, the institution's representatives have sometimes hesitated to agree to meet with the review team, but in all cases thus far, they ultimately have done so and have felt the process was salutary. A principle problem accounting for this hesitation is a basic lack of information about mediation. Most parties do not fully understand the differences among mediation, arbitration, and litigation. Explanations must be made to the effect that the informal, flexible nature of mediation allows parties to discuss potential solutions without admitting fault or guilt, that mediation results in self-generated solutions, rather than those imposed by a third party, and that, if mediation fails, the parties generally have access to more formal remedial measures.

When the review team visits the campus to meet with institutional representatives, usually in the office of the president, the team may find the institution's attorney present and a tape recorder in the room. If asked whether AAUA has any objection to the attorney's participating in the discussions, the team explains that there is no objection whatsoever, since the meeting has no legal significance and AAUA has no enforcement or sanctioning authority. The team is interested only in knowing how the facts of the situation relate to AAUA Standards, and whether or not there is sufficient information to indicate that the Standards may not have been met. The matter of the tape recorder is handled in a similar fashion: there is no objection to the discussion being recorded, but the information gathered at the meeting will be typed and sent back to the institutional representatives for correction and verification before it becomes part of any AAUA report. Usually the institutional representatives accept this explanation, the attorney is sent away, and the tape recorder is turned off. As AAUA's goal of helping the parties themselves reach an amicable solution becomes clear to the institutional representatives, they usually are cooperative in supplying as much information as possible.

The overarching strategy used by the review team is to refocus the attention of the parties away from personal concerns and toward professional ones, since AAUA's interest is the furtherance of professionalism in higher education administration. The tactic of gathering facts and asking that they be verified by both parties forces a definition of the professional problem. In the course of defining the problem, new language may be used to describe what happened, a reformulation of the issue may occur, and an internal solution may be facilitated by providing the parties with facts upon which they can see they agree, including how the misunderstanding began and why it happened. Sometimes, however, a team may enter a dispute on one ground and then find that the concerns enlarge. For example, the problem may seem procedural regarding the termination of a single administrator, but the underlying problem may be substantial, involving poorly defined internal administrative responsibilities or difficulties between the institution and a state or federal agency. In one notable case, a team began to mediate a dispute among a president, a governing board, a faculty senate, and a faculty union. Very soon it was asked to broaden its inquiry to look at attempts being made by community officials, citizens, and press to influence day-to-day decision making at the college. The team eventually was successful in helping these various groups sort out their appropriate roles. When several levels of concerns emerge, the team looks first to those to which the parties can react as professionals, in order to reestablish useful lines of communication. The team may spend more time on resolving issues that will affect the future rather than the present, in order to prevent the same problem from arising again in similar circumstances. In addition, the team may serve as brokers by putting the parties in touch with other persons or groups that may be helpful in achieving a settlement.

Third Step: Review. Step Three of the process is a formal review. It occurs only if the AAUA team has not successfully helped the parties reach agreement at Step Two. The team then prepares a written factual summary of its findings and submits a copy to all disputants for verification or challenge. When it receives replies from them and clarifies the report in light of these responses, it sends the chairperson of the Standards and Review Committee a verified summary of the facts, along with the team's recommendation for a solution.

The Standards and Review Committee then develops its own recommendations,which are sent to the AAUA President with a file consisting of a copy of the verified summary of facts, the recommendation of the AAUA team, and the recommendations of the Standards and Review Committee regarding a solution and a final report. In turn, the AAUA President, after consulting with the AAUA General Secretary, General Counsel, and Chairperson of Standards and Review, forwards the whole package to the AAUA Board of Directors as the body that determines official AAUA action. The Board may direct the AAUA President or other AAUA official to make one more attempt to mediate the remaining differences; it may accept the final report and direct that it be published or be made available upon request to AAUA members who are considering employment at the institution; and it may indicate to the parties AAUA's willingness to be invited back to the campus to see the results of the review team's work and of interim measures accepted by the parties in resolving the dispute.

Settlements effected by AAUA do not result in signed agreements between the parties, as in some forms of mediation. Instead, by the end of the mediation process, a series of actions usually has taken place, such as providing an accurate letter of recommendation and agreeing to certain compensation for a terminated administrator, or has begun, such as the drafting of new institutional policies and procedures. This feature of a settlement may continue long after the concerns of the particular individual are met and illustrates AAUA's dual concerns—the needs of the individual and those of the institution and the profession. AAUA inability to achieve such settlements usually results from one of the parties feeling that their actions have met its Standards and that they have taken all reasonable steps necessary for settlement. Sometimes a lawsuit or administrative agency complaint is then filed by the other party. In the course of that action, AAUA may be called upon to provide an expert witness regarding custom and practice within the profession.

Users of AAUA's Mediation Service

As noted earlier, AAUA's mediation service is available regarding alleged violations of its Standards affecting individual administrators, institutions, or others, whether or not they belong to AAUA. Of the administrators who have sought AAUA's assistance, deans make up the largest group, followed in numbers by vice-presidents, presidents, directors, provosts, division heads, and chairpersons. Most cases have involved the academic affairs area, followed by student affairs, the presidential office, the business office, and the planning staff in order of frequency. Most administrators who have asked for assistance have been employed at public four-year institutions. Next in frequency are public graduate-level institutions, two-year community colleges, religious four-year schools, and, last, private nonsectarian four-year institutions.

Selection of Mediators

AAUA mediators are selected by its Standards and Review Committee from among administrators with great personal experience and success in academic administration, including presidents, vice-presidents, and deans of professional schools. The Committee attempts to match the competencies of the mediator or mediators with the characteristics of the situation. For instance, if a dean or president at a public four-year institution in involved, the AAUA review team will involve persons of at least the same rank and with experience at similar institutions. However, an attempt is made to comprise a team with various competencies; thus in addition to including people whose characteristics broadly match those of individuals involved directly in the case, others on the team will reflect views from the different vantage points of other kinds of institutions, or foundations and higher education organizations. The intention is for the assembled competencies represented by the team to make accessible to the parties a wide range of possible alternatives for finding an amicable solution to the problem. The parties to the dispute are not involved in the selection of mediators, and they cannot veto team members. It is noteworthy, however, that so far no mediator has been held unacceptable by the parties to a dispute. In fact, a number of mediators, having concluded the particular assignment for which they were appointed, have been asked to return to handle another issue that arose subsequently, and individuals who were the "other party" in a case have later initiated calls to AAUA regarding new problems.

Costs Associated with AAUA Mediation

The costs associated with mediation are minimal compared to more formal methods of dispute settlement, such as arbitration, agency adjudication, or litigation. The amount of time spent in mediating a dispute usually is substantially less, so that even when legal counsel is assisting in mediating, there are fewer hours spent than in other situations. The principal costs, normally, are the travel expenses of the mediators. The Association reimburses team members for these expenses, while the team members donate their time through their own generosity and that of their institutions. This degree of volunteer service by administrators and institutions is a solid indication of the worth attributed to mediation by the mediators and their institutions.

The costs associated with the AAUA mediation service are at present largely absorbed by the Association. To date, persons requesting assistance have not been assessed costs, but AAUA is currently considering the following charges: In investigating requests for assistance, AAUA's services would be free to AAUA members after six months' membership. Nonmembers and AAUA members of less than six months would be charged up to 3 percent of their annual institutional salary for the cost of investigation. And institutions that request an AAUA investigation would be charged its full cost.

Reactions of the Parties to the Process

AAUA's experience in mediating disputes involving its Standards has led to the strong conviction that the offer of assistance from administrative colleagues carries two powerful incentives: the value of an outsider's eye, combined with a set of educational values likely to be compatible with those of all of the parties involved in the particular problem. The outsider, in effect, comes to be trusted because he or she is actually an "insider," albeit from another institution or educational setting.

That this trust develops is substantiated by the reactions of the parties to the AAUA mediation process. Among the comments from complainants is the following: "I want to express my appreciation for all the help you gave regarding my settlement . . . . Your specific suggestions as well as your general encouragement certainly helped me through a difficult situation. I can now feel good about it all being behind me, and I am in an excellent position professionally for now and for the future." Another administrator wrote, "I am grateful for the time and effort, as well as the rich thought, that the AAUA and you, as their representative, have expended on this matter . . . . To come directly to the point, let me say that the situation has been honestly met and happily resolved during the past summer."

Institutions have been reassured by AAUA's insistence that administrators exhaust all internal remedies before resorting to requesting assistance from AAUA, and they have thus been encouraged to have in place sufficient procedures so that their autonomy need not be breached by interventions from outside.

Not all of those requesting assistance have sympathized with AAUA's requirement regarding prior exhaustion of internal remedies. One dean whose institution wanted to buy out his contract and who refused even to attempt to exhaust internal remedies, wrote, "You talk about exhaustion. I cannot see how anything can be more 'exhausted' . . . . What a laugh!" And the voluntary consent needed to conduct mediation has also come under criticism from persons requesting assistance. Another dean wrote, "What assistance can you offer? [An] *attempt* to negotiate with my president . . . is an empty and rather useless gesture." Nonetheless, successful settlements are reached in most cases, according to reports from the parties involved.

Among the prime elements in successful settlements are rescuing administrators' professional reputations, negotiating termination pay, vacation pay, and similar monetary compensation for losses suffered due to arbitrary and capricious action, and improving existing but deficient institutional policies and procedures for future use. From the individual administrator's viewpoint, the most common acceptable solution is the restoration of his or her professional reputation. Seldom are administrators sanguine about the prospect of being reinstated in the post which they held, and, indeed, they rarely are reinstated. Rather, they wish to search for new posts from the strongest possible position. They are concerned that they have an accurate letter of recommendation in their personnel file, and institutions are generally agreeable to providing such letters. In addition, administrators usually suffer monetary losses because of arbitrary actions taken against them. Successful settlements often include payment of salary for the period of time remaining in a contract or in the year, as well as vacation pay, severance pay, insurance coverage, and children's tuition remission. Arrangements sometimes are also made for the individual's use of an interim title, office, telephone, and similar assistance in seeking another position.

From the institution's point of view, the identification of areas where its policies and procedures are inadequate is a valuable by-product of the mediation process. Successful settlements often result in institutions implementing new policies or following lapsed policies in areas of administrators' employment, career considerations, and personal responsibilities, and in administrative office operations. For example, institutions may adopt policies that provide for written contracts, periodic evaluation and review, specific dates for notification of action regarding renewal or termination, and stated responsibilities of office. In holding that due process is a flexible concept that may take a slightly different form at different institutions, AAUA Standards do not specify a particular period of notice of termination or renewal, such as nine months or a year. Instead, they encourage regular evaluation of each individual's job performance, provision of this information to the individual about the institution's view of this performance, and reasonable notice of termination in terms of finding new employment. A termination occurring in line with such policies and procedures seldom would be viewed by AAUA as arbitrary or capricious.

Two kinds of negative comments about AAUA mediation do not pertain directly to the mediators or the mediation process. The first, noted earlier, involves AAUA's requirement that internal remedies be exhausted before AAUA enters the case. Some persons believe that such prior exhaustion at a particular institution is an exercise in futility, but AAUA is firm in encouraging settlement of disputes at the institutional level, if at all possible, before intervening. The second involves the assertion that AAUA moves too slowly. This complaint may well be justified at times, although AAUA operates as expeditiously as possible, considering the fact that its mediators volunteer their services, and some situations simply are plagued with more scheduling difficulties and time commitment problems than others.

When AAUA is able to achieve a settlement, the parties generally agree that success is due to the review team's ability to focus their attention on objective issues and to depersonalize their dispute. No longer is it a case of one party versus another, but of two parties being asked to join together in assembling a set of facts and seeing how these facts measure up to an objective set of professional standards. Seeking an amicable solution is emphasized, not placing blame or imposing a sanction. Threats are replaced by a process that allows the parties to regain a collegial stance—if not toward one another, at least toward a common concern for the profession of higher education administration.

Mediation in the 1980s

The growth of AAUA's mediation service each year since it became operational is evidence that as institutions and individuals learn about it, they make use of it. Yet so far there has been relatively little publicity about the service due to its very nature. It is designed to settle issues at the institutional level, to allow parties to formulate remedies which are satisfactory to them without outside publicity, and to permit institutions to change their policies and operations without being held up to censure for past inadequacies.

As we move into the 1980s, with the stresses created by diminishing economic resources, AAUA anticipates a substantial increase in requests for assistance. As already indicated, AAUA undertakes mediation only when an institution's policies are not in compliance with AAUA Standards. But AAUA assistance may be of even greater benefit to the institution and its administrators at other times, as when they find themselves facing issues with which they lack experience or familiarity, such as financial crisis, institutional reorganization, presidential search and selection, accreditation reviews, federal or state regulation compliance, disputes with internal governance bodies such as faculty senates or student governing bodies, and incidents involving the student press, collective bargaining agents, or various groups outside the institution. AAUA recognizes that mediation may be a useful process in handling such situations. At the same time, the notion that mediation is a sign of failure or incompetence has diminished. Administrators are coming to see mediation in higher education as a new tool of dispute resolution that provides a combination of autonomy and innovation in a setting in which educational values play a major role.

Concern for the quality of its services looms large as a factor in AAUA's consideration of its willingness to broaden its mediation aid beyond cases involving its Standards. There is no question that mediation is effective in settling disputes where these Standards serve as a benchmark to measure professionalism. AAUA believes that the same success will follow in disputes where some other superordinate goal can be substituted for its Standards. It appears likely that a wide variety of matters in academia are appropriate to settlement by mediation. The principal issues seem to be to inform educators about the value of mediation, to find mechanisms to cover its costs, and to expand its benefits without compromising its quality. In this process, AAUA hopes to serve not only its members but the profession of academic administration and higher education at large.

*Patricia A. Hollander is general counsel for the American Association
of University Administrators, and a consultant and lecturer on
legal issues in higher education. She is author of the* Legal Handbook
for Educators.

Conflict between president and governing board or within the governing board can be reduced through informal third-party intervention.

Resolving Conflict in the Upper Echelons

J. L. Zwingle

Other chapters in this *New Directions* sourcebook describe conflict involving faculty, students, administrators, and government agencies that may be alleviated by some version of formal mediation. This chapter examines other conflicts that may be even more damaging to an institution but, at the same time, less open to third-party mediation: those between the governing board and the president and among members of the governing board itself.

In discussing this swampy terrain with friends and colleagues, I have found little encouragement for mediation. Some of them seem to suppose that in such conflicts the outcome is comparable to the classic Greek tragedy, with something built into the situation or into the persons themselves that inevitably determines the final scene. Perhaps so; but let us not admit the inevitability of tragedy without considering other possibilities.

Board-President Relationships

The presidency of a college or university has always been at best hazardous, but today the presidency has become more and more demanding, the pressures greater, and the charms of office even less attractive than in former days. Among presidents who resigned the office in a recent year, the reason they most often mentioned was differences with the governing board (Cole, 1976). Without going into the details of the kinds of differences which led to the separation, one faces a curious paradox: The president is a person chosen by the board, surely on the assumption that this person was qualified for the office. The choice is usually made after a difficult and painstaking search. How does it come about then that a person so carefully chosen by a board made up of such experienced and perceptive persons turns out to be deficient? In the face of such reversals, what is one to conclude? Surely the vast researches of social science should give us a clue. Until that happy time does come, it is at least sensible to take a look at the problem and to cultivate a few long thoughts about it.

Let us begin with one basic fact: that frequent changes in the central administration, particularly in the presidency, are enormously expensive to the institution both in direct and in indirect costs. If it should prove possible to rescue a sinking president, great might be the savings. To be sure, there are terminal cases that must be terminated. But termination is not necessarily the cure in all cases, perhaps not even in most. At least one consultant intimately known to me has said to more than one board, "A vacancy in the president's office may be necessary, but the basic problem of the institution will still be with you."

The Possibility of Third-Party Mediation

When and how could mediation improve such situations? Before answering that question, one must look closely at the nature of the problem. Perhaps we can take for granted that the special nature of the academy as an organization is recognized by all. The remaining issue is whether within the academy the trustee-president connection is itself something different from related problems outside the academy. One who looks back on decades of experience in various kinds of organizations and institutions may be tempted to come flat out with declarations.

But let us not fall into quick generalizations. Let us try to creep up on the problem this way: assume at the outset something of a first proposition, that in a heavy conflict between board and president, both parties are competent and that the situation is potentially reversible. Otherwise, third-party efforts would be foolish, unless of course the third-party can expedite and lubricate the inevitable changes—changes not alone in the occupant of the president's chair but possibly also a few changes of personnel (or practice) in the board.

To understand the problem still further, ask what is the principal obstruction. First of all, it is pride of position. For the president it is a self-contradiction to think that a third-party is needed. Presidents by definition are expected to be able to understand everything that is going on and to know what to do—evidence to the contrary notwithstanding. For the trustee-regent, the same pride of position leads to considerable self-confidence and self-deception. The very fact of becoming a trustee/regent symbolizes a level of distinction and competence, and the members themselves are likely to accept their supposed competence without misgiving. Successes achieved elsewhere are falsely supposed to be immediately transferable to the boardroom. It may be true for some, but certainly not for all, and not for every occasion. Given these prior assumptions it is little wonder that boardrooms of every kind are supercharged with an ego factor beyond compare. Restraint and humility are not commonplace virtues of human beings generally, but the boardroom is a kind of hothouse where the ego can blossom to the full, as hardly anywhere else, both in the executive and the board member.

Another aspect of the self-perception of the trustee: some board members are engaged in enterprises much greater in scope than those of the college or university. For such persons the administrative concerns of a campus may seem picayune, and even more particularly the typical concerns of the faculty or the students. Yet still other trustees may have a different role outside the boardroom. For some, trusteeship is the principal outlet. Such a mixture of backgrounds and motivations provides a special challenge to a president. A prime responsibility of the office is to cultivate and elevate a board which on one hand he answers to and on the other hand he must help to enliven and develop. In this mixture of types among board members there will inevitably be found certain centers of power, persons who are the acknowledged leaders and deciders. When two or more persons aspire to this position, they and their respective followers can form opposing forces to the ultimate distress of the institution, not alone the president. Even when the power goes unchallenged, whether it be trustee power or presidential power, the result will ultimately be unfortunate. Constant challenge is itself destructive. Yet one or another of these extremes characterize many an institution.

The reader who is now disturbed by the foregoing comments should wait a bit longer before turning aside. What has been said may sound like just another condemnation of trusteeship in general. Not so. Trusteeship should be judged not by abstract standards of perfection but by realistic comparison with alternatives. One who has spent years working with volunteers of every type in various sorts of organizations and situations can but testify to the value of voluntary trusteeship, and to its still unrealized potential. Defects of trusteeship can certainly not be remedied by turning to governmental agencies or to purely professional management. Here, as elsewhere, the question is how to improve the system, especially how to deal with internal crises which threaten the enterprise and the institutions of postsecondary education.

Now let us turn to some typical situations and ponder the feasibility of something akin to mediation. As noted elsewhere in these chapters, the term "mediation" is a poor one to use in connection with presidents and trustees — as well as for others in the academy. But let us not be hampered by semantics. Instead let us project a possible arrangement which could accomplish the needed result. So now a few words about atmosphere and preconditions: How confidential? How private? Like all fairly closed systems, a campus is great for flashes of rumor and floods of hearsay. But a degree of privacy and confidentiality can be achieved when those are urgent requirements. Decision on that point must come early or it will be everlastingly too late. Some situations, however, require considerable public exposure from the start, which is another judgment to be made. In either case the consultation (rather than mediation) must be shaped up well at the outset. Neither president nor board is likely to agree to formal mediation. Both, however, are likely to accept consultation which must ultimately leave to the parties whether or not findings will be accepted. Each party may have announced hard positions admitting of no retreat. What then is to be accomplished? In some instances it may be that the very process of consultation will result in softened attitudes. The process of consultation tends to make more objective the matters which tend to become highly subjective. In this process, it becomes possible to define anew the conditions which hold the best promise for the total institution—a goal which both parties must perforce accept. Then as both parties testify about the complex of issues there will almost certainly emerge some basis for action without undue loss of face, or with a reasonable distribution of humble pie.

Almost certainly the core of the problem, after all else is put aside, will be the question of power and authority (these matters are frequently bound up in conflicts of personality). In a contest of power, it is possible to demonstrate that the demonstration of final authority seldom solves a problem. The correct decision about when to assert authority requires the most refined judgment, a sure sense of the factors involved, and the proper timing. Assertion of authority in a way that is perceived to be contrary to the well-being of the institution will surely worsen the situation. On the contrary, a board or president that shrinks from responsibility when decisive action is needed will worsen the situation. It is just the ability to exercise good judgment which is most needed in trustees and presidents alike. Third-party consultation holds the possibility of refining the judgment required, provided the outside advice is sought early enough. All too frequently consultation is sought only when controversy has reached white-heat, a point when even heroic effort may only save portions of the situation or a few of the persons.

In seeking ways to resolve conflicts between a board and a president, the key persons are chairman and other officers of the board. If both parties appear to be locked in total disagreement, someone should begin by asking some specially chosen trustee (or two or three) to take initiative informally, with the objective of identifying anew the central issues in the controversy and selecting meticulously some specific point at which conversation may become objective, insisting that the well-being of the institution serve as the standard for discussion. Then, with the possible assistance of a third party, it may prove possible to broaden the chosen single issue into a larger context of discussion. In talking with a third party, a careful review of the history of the controversy may surprise the participants with a sense of new perspective. All this may seem too obvious, but experience has demonstrated how even at late stages of controversy the sense of new perspective or at least a reduction in hostility can be achieved.

Typical Situations

The Finance Dilemma. The term *finance* covers a large area with many subdivisions, each one hazardous in some special way. A maxim with an element of truth says that a president who is successful in financial management will be forgiven anything else. Financial management begins with income. A strong, steady flow of money will cover a multitude of defects, but money always has a source, and sometimes a price. The president is the central character in dealing with sources and in deciding when the price becomes too high.

For state-related institutions, the principal source is the legislature. For these institutions, the most sensitive relationships are likely to be those affecting legislators and the governor of the state. Presidents who have enjoyed long tenure in such institutions have uniformly been those who sustained effective working relations with the state capitol. When that relationship goes sour, the hope of recovery depends entirely on the kind of mediation exercised. It can take many forms. Both the president and the state officials need a few honest brokers, so to speak, who understand both the proper functions of the university and the realities of the political system. The landscape is littered with wreckage from failures on one side or the other in this style of controversy. The history of such failures can be found in state after state. It is of course commonplace for state-related institutions to have experienced personnel who deal with the state government, and most of the time this system works well enough. But there are special occasions when disaster threatens, and at such times special measures are needed. While state relations form a constant part of the agenda, it would be hard to demonstrate that institutions without a contingency plan designed for emergencies have an adequate approach to the annual struggle for appropriations. Too frequently it is only in crises that the need for some special resources is recognized.

Much the same thing could be said for the private institution, except that there is seldom one major central source of funds. Major donors have been known to prove intractable, as have alumni, corporations, and perhaps others who threaten a cut-off in support unless this or that be done. Staff members of many an institution have been through storm and stress over relations with these sources. Fortunately there are available within the ranks of the institution (on campus or off) persons who do a great deal of successful mediation on behalf of the administration, usually through successful improvisation rather than a procedure formulated in advance. Missing in most institutions, public or private, is a number of well-prepared, competent intermediaries for support and protection of the institution in times of difficulty.

The Divided Board. Conflicts within governing boards are almost inevitable, and they arise from every imaginable kind of issue—from the selection of a president to problems of unpopular or controversial teachers, student recruitment, athletics, and any number of other issues. Controversy is in itself not altogether bad if it leads to clarification and ultimate settlement of policy; but quarrelsomeness and continued vendettas are a drain on the energies of board and staff alike, and a substantial cost to the institution. Such conflicts within the board have characterized many an institution, from the largest to the smallest, public and private. Some presidents, by personal skill and good luck, have managed such conflicts successfully and have not themselves been unduly scarred, but they are exceptional. Others have maintained office by outlasting or outwitting first one and then another set of opponents, holding on by whatever means possible but not truly managing or leading their institutions. Meanwhile the board members are caught up in moves and countermoves which intensify neglect of the longer-term welfare of the institution. When one counts the number of places suffering from unresolved differences within boards, one is drawn to the conclusion that systematic third-party consultation (qua mediation) could accomplish a good result.

The Domineering Individual. Many an institution has been severely damaged because some person chose to play the role of power center. This personality type is to be found at all levels and in all types of organizations. But in the academy, especially when it is a trustee who is involved, the price is usually high. The question was once raised about a board chairman who made it a practice to contact faculty members by telephone, asking questions and issuing instructions. A good answer to such a situation would be for the faculty member to state that he or she would take action such on such fiats only when informed in writing that such calls had been authorized by the full board, or at any rate to insist on written communications to which he or she would then make written replies. That response would almost certainly stop the calls.

To be sure, a president can play the domineering role. If such a president is also productive, the board may choose to give way, reap the benefits, and avoid friction. Ultimately however, the board will pay a price when seeking that president's successor, because the board will either be too weak and inexperienced in trusteeship, or it will overcorrect its past demeanor before testing itself under true responsibility.

The question remains whether any kind of third-party function can restrain and redirect the energies of the offending person(s). Here we have a complex and elusive problem. When the offending person is a member of the board, who will take the initiative in this project of remonstrance? If one inquires why a board will submit, as some are known to do, to the arrogation of power by one or more persons, the answer may not come easily, although foremost among possible explanations is the fact that in a group of volunteers hardly anyone cares to incur the kind of unpleasantness sure to follow a challenge to a powerful fellow member.

Such confrontations can be harrowing indeed, fraught with potent potential damage to other relationships, and when no great principle is at stake there
is temptation to let things go their own way. If, however, a board has two or
more contenders for center stage the boardroom will become an arena and the
agenda will be secondary to the personal contests.

Anyone who has observed episodes where challenges to assume power
have been been made will know that distraction from personality disputes is
effected through the painful persistence of a few who see the larger issues. Often
the outcome will be left to the passage of time and a quiet hope for an upturn in
events. If it is supposed that situations of this sort are too rare to warrant space
in this discussion, the reader has been spared a great deal. From state to state,
from institution to institution, a list of boardrooms suffering in just this fashion
would be long indeed. But timely action together with persistence can work a
constructive change and a reduction of damage when neutral but qualified persons initiate third-party efforts. If neither an officer of the board nor a committee chairman will take the initiative, any member of the board is free to try. The
first step is merely to find two or three others who agree on the need for action,
and then enlist the most available person of influence. Ultimately, it should be
possible for a plan to emerge to enlist qualified persons from outside, who then
can in due course and with all due precaution develop options which can be
informally discussed and evaluated by the parties at interest. If these efforts
ultimately fall short, at least the situation will have been clarified and the possibility of final resolution will have been improved.

The Special Interest Syndrome. Here is one that takes many forms,
some relatively harmless, others potentially devastating. The more harmless
ones come in the form of hobbyists. The hobby may be almost any sort of activity which some avid group thinks would enhance the institution. Such groups
may well be encouraged, as long as their activities do not divert any department
from its main purpose. The more dangerous special interest takes the form of
commercial or industrial invasion of the institution, threatening exploitation
of one or another department — or indeed, the entire institution. Proposals come
in various forms, some legitimate on the surface, some all but fantastic; some
accompanied by money, others only with prospects. In any case they are invi-
tations to controversy. The appeal is quite natural. Institutions are offered the
prospect of financial gain, of enlarged constituency, of improved public relations. Often someone within the close constituency of the institution will be the
promoter or supporter of the project, urging prompt action lest the opportunity
be lost. Included here must also be those arrangements whereby a member of
the board (or of the administration or faculty) may incur a conflict of interest.
Although institutions are now adopting policies to cover these conflicts, it is not
always easy to judge. Early invitation to third-party review can avoid the pain
of later disagreements.

The Breakdown in Confidence. No doubt someone will say that this
is one category too many. How could anybody suppose that a third-party effort

could do anything about such a generalized condition as "breakdown in confidence?" A case could be made that when there is loss of confidence in the president, it is a terminal disease. Perhaps. But there are instances of supposedly terminal diseases that were arrested, and health restored.

So-called loss of confidence may occasionally be plain unpopularity. It is misleading to suppose that unpopularity is the equivalent of either being wrong or being forever ineffective. Several long-term, effective presidents have never enjoyed a great wave of personal popularity. The source of a reported loss of confidence may also turn out to be rather limited in the number of people to which that report accurately applies. Administrators clearly go through periods of ebb and flow in their relations with various groups in the academy. The faculty may be outraged by some action recommended by the president and supported by the board. It is, of course, a serious matter when a faculty votes "no confidence," but such a vote need not be considered the final stroke. Careful analysis of the reasons for the vote, the history of the problem, and its relation to realistic long-term institutional policy can lead to a conclusion other than that the president is finished. The symptom which appears in the form of "loss of confidence" may in fact be a symptom of other and larger problems.

Whatever the degree and extent of the supposed loss of confidence, it is a matter in which some form of third-party function might prove valuable to everyone. Unfortunately, however, one finds a degree of cynicism (or fatalism) about presidents — that they are expendable, persons who at best may be able to accomplish some good things over a short span but who (perhaps like athletes) have a predictably short life-expectancy on the job. In weighing this important aspect of institutional life, one can observe a certain gamesmanship. Presidents have been known to be quick at playing the "confidence issue," sometimes making even minor matters appear as implicit symbols of confidence or no-confidence. It is a game in which even winners are losers after a certain run.

In addition, various problems of public relations and of internal relations play into the area of "confidence." One of the more familiar controversies within this general category is reaction to proposed changes in curriculum, structure, organization, emphasis — all those elements making up an established pattern of a college or university. Not a few presidents have been personal victims of this kind of resistance even when changes were sought by the board and may even been the basis on which the president was chosen. New programs accompanied by new funds have been known to light the fires of opposition. But it is more often the opposite which rallies the troops, something more familiar to our time: retrenchment. This is a task that calls for the ultimate in human resources, and perforce it involves both the board and the president as the final locus of decision. Third-party efforts can certainly achieve much in situations of this kind (and better before than after), for one or more third parties will likely be involved before the resolution, and those not of the president's choosing or else outside his sphere of control.

It is safe to say that at no time will elements in an institution be fine-tuned, right on pitch. It is safe to say that at any time of the year, something will be amiss; but the basic issue is more general: whether the institution has strong vital signs, whether it is essentially dynamic. That can best be ascertained by observing trend lines for all the essential functions, and realistic reading of the short-term outlook.

To return to the question of the third-party role when the loss of confidence issue arises, many an issue has been analyzed and set straight in the normal course of business between presidents and trustees/regents. Skillful presidents and board members will eventually work out a system by which threatened disruption can be identified and forestalled. Obviously not all presidents and board members are adequately skillful in this way, and hence a greater willingness to utilize some third-party resource would bespeak wiser institutional management. This suggestion need not be thought of as depicting a state of constant alert, a squad of specialists poised for the next alarm. In the issue of confidence in the administration, as in other types of institutional stress, boards too often conclude that changing presidents is the inevitable solution. Before reaching this conclusion, trustees/regents would do well to seek the best available outside analysts to help clarify the issues and, circumstances and people permitting, identify possible alternative courses.

Summary

In naming a few broad categories of conflict which involve the highest echelons of the academy, we have not tried to be exhaustive. Essentially, we have attempted to remind the reader of certain familiar types of conflict that have seriously damaged institutions but which might have turned out differently (and better) if there had been timely resort to qualified third-party advice and recommendations. Much of what has been suggested would perhaps come under the heading of maintenance, if such high-level functionaries could suppose that they are indeed not always self-correcting nor always adequately prepared for the judgment which they eventually must render. We know to our cost that airplanes and nuclear reactors require close inspection and ready correction, the hazards are great and the results of negligence are often fatal. In the more slow-moving world of the academy, the maintenance procedures are not so easily described or performed. In fact, the academy is less like a machine, more like a plant, an organism that is either growing or dying, so the question is one of environment, of nutrients, of cultivation. When one considers how many factors must work correctly and simultaneously within human institutions if they are to succeed, it is a wonder that things proceed as well as they do. In the past great dependence has been placed on institutions of learning, and a great deal has been accomplished. In the days ahead it remains to be seen whether for these important social institutions ways can be found to reduce human cost and to enhance institutional vigor. Presidents and their boards, or boards and their presidents, might gain by trying a new approach to solve some very old problems.

J. L. Zwingle is an author and consultant in higher education, the former president of Park College in Missouri, and former vice-president for planning and development at Cornell University. He is also a past president of the Association of Governing Boards.

*Appeal procedures at the University of Michigan illustrate one way
institutions can protect student interests and assure due process
for students.*

Handling Student Grievances in Higher Education

Janelle Shubert
Joseph Folger

Over the last two decades colleges and universities have begun to reexamine the
implementation of their internal rules and regulations. Although these procedures were once largely autonomous and idiosyncratic, recent legislation,
judicial decisions, and federal regulations have more narrowly specified the
issues that internal policies must address and have also encouraged the development of more formal enforcement and evaluation procedures. One area of higher
education where the impact of these developments has been particularly significant is that of student rights.

Historical Impetus

Prior to the 1960s few institutions of higher education had adopted disciplinary action codes that provided a student with a hearing in cases of dismissal, charges of dishonesty, or violation of institutional regulations. During the
campus riots in the 1960s, many students were disciplined, or subjected to legal
prosecution. As Edwards and Nordin (1979) note, these actions challenged
basic assumptions regarding the "privilege versus right" to education issue,
the interpretation of *in loco parentis,* and the institution's right of exclusive

jurisdiction over students. Given the tenor of the times and the issues being debated, it is not surprising that student consumerism increased and that students themselves began to seek redress for their grievances in the courts.

One outcome of these combined events was the design and adoption of disciplinary procedures which, as they evolved, acknowledged and granted due process to students. At first, however, granting due process involved little more than the minimum right to hear or receive charges and the right to request a hearing.

The passage of a series of federal regulations and guidelines for grievance hearings broadened the grounds on which students could seek redress for alleged violation of their rights. These regulations included:

- *Executive Order 11246* prohibiting discrimination in employment on the basis of race, color, religion, sex and national origin by all federal government contractors.
- *Title VI of the Civil Rights Act of 1964* prohibiting exclusion from, participation in, denial of benefits and discrimination under federally assisted programs on the basis of race, color or national origin.
- *Title IX of the Education Amendments of 1972* prohibiting educational institutions that receive federal funds from discrimination on the basis of sex.
- *Buckley Amendment* (Family Educational Rights and Privacy Act, 1974) regulating and limiting the use to be made of information in students' files.
- *Rehabilitation Act of 1973 Section 504* prohibiting by sole reason of handicap the exclusion of individuals from participation in or the benefits of any program or activity receiving federal financial assistance.

As a result of regulations developed to implement these acts, students were no longer restricted to answering charges brought against them, nor did they have to rely on judicial proceedings to air their grievances, They now had available to them, at the institutional level, mechanisms for airing their grievances.

In addition to the federal regulations and guidelines for hearing grievances, decisions rendered in state, district, and Supreme Court cases have also encouraged the development of academic grievance procedures. Among the most significant judicial decisions were those which (1) established the parameters for student action by applying the contract or quasi-contract theory of law, (2) addressed the issue of due process and procedural due process, and (3) affirmed the courts' position on academic abstention. These decisions mean that while colleges and universities retain their right to internal governance in academic matters, this governance must now reflect the individual's constitutional rights or risk litigation.

Beginning in the mid 1960s, various national education associations

began to urge colleges and universities to institute some form of student grievance procedures. The *Statement on Government of Colleges and Universities* drafted
between 1964 and 1966 by the American Association of University Professors,
the American Council on Education, and the Association of Governing Boards,
calls on colleges and universities to afford students "the right to academic due
process when charged with serious violations of institutional regulations." And
in June 1971 the Carnegie Commission on Higher Education issued its report
on *Dissent and Disruption: Proposals for Consideration by the Campus* that contained
a detailed model "Bill of Rights and Responsibilities for Members of the Institution: Faculty, Students, Administrators, Staff, and Trustees." In 1979 the
American Council on Education formed a self-regulatory task force that published a proposed code of fair practices, including a call for student grievance
procedures, and in the same year the Carnegie Council on Policy Studies in
Higher Education published *Fair Practices in Higher Education,* a report recommending that colleges and universities "develop equitable, easily navigable, and
publicized grievance procedures." The report cited Joan Stark's guidelines in
The Many Faces of Educational Consumerism as a basis for the procedures.

How have colleges and universities responded to these recommendations? Because the existence of student grievance procedures is relatively new,
we know very little about how individual institutions have gone about designing
and implementing them. However, since these procedures are closely tied to
federal regulatory compliance, and to the court's interpretation of the role of
higher education, it is critical that as much information as possible be made
available to aid institutions as they enact these student appeals procedures.

For purposes of illustration this chapter describes the student grievance
procedures that have been adopted by the School of Graduate Studies at the
University of Michigan, and the experience the University has had in using
both the formal and the informal mechanisms of handling complaints.

University of Michigan Student Grievance Procedures

The University of Michigan has adopted both formal and informal processes for resolving student initiated grievances. Because of the size of the University and its decentralized system of administration, grievances (both for
undergraduates and graduate students) are typically handled first at the departmental or unit level. Decisions made at that level may then be appealed to the
college or school. While these procedures include the right to take action on
the basis of alleged discrimination (sex, race, or handicap status), the University
also has procedures whereby students may file a grievance through the Office
of Affirmative Action, independent of the academic grievance procedures.

One example of grievance procedures available to students above the
departmental level are those which are used in the Horace H. Rackham School
of Graduate Studies at the University of Michigan. Instituted in 1976, the pro-

cedures are intended for students registered in the Graduate School or for graduate students in other schools who have requested a change of venue. The procedures allow for the review of a grievance on academic matters. This includes grading, evaluation or status, claims by students that they have been denied access to their records or that data in those records has been used inappropriately, student claims that there has been professional misconduct toward them or that they have been treated unfairly or in a discriminatory way. Students may also seek review of disciplinary action taken against them or about allegedly unfair or improper rules, regulations, policies or procedures.

Graduate students who have a grievance on any of the above grounds are required to attempt a resolution of the grievance at the departmental or unit level. If they are dissatisfied with the decision at that level, they may then bring the grievance to the Graduate School Referee.

The role of the Referee is to give initial advice to the student about both informal and formal processes available for resolving the grievance. First and foremost, the Referee tries to mediate the grievance informally with the department or other agency. If this is unsuccessful, the student may initiate a formal written appeal, and the Referee then conducts a hearing and makes the first ruling on behalf of the Graduate School.

If a student or faculty member is dissatisfied with the decision of the Referee, or if the Referee disqualifies herself, the appeal then goes to the Graduate School Appeals Panel. This panel is composed of eight members of the graduate faculty (appointed by the Dean and Executive Board for a term of three years) and four graduate students (appointed by the Rackham Student Government for a one-year term.) The Panel may refuse to accept an appeal if it determines that the issue is not actionable under the procedures or if it determines that, "on the basis of the facts stated by the grievant, viewed in the light most favorable to the grievant, there is no basis for relief." When the Panel is notified that an appeal has been initiated or transferred to it, the Secretary of the Panel notifies both parties of the names and positions of the Panel members eligible to serve on a Hearing Board. Each of the disputants selects one member of the Panel to serve on the Hearing Board, and these two choose a third. Parties are then notified of the date for a hearing and the rules for conducting such a hearing. On the basis of information presented in the hearing, the Board makes a decision which contains the findings of fact, the decision, reasons for the decision, and the policy basis or criteria applied in reaching the decision. The decision of the Board is final and it can affirm, reverse or modify the decision of the Referee.

Throughout the entire grievance procedure, from the departmental level through a full Board hearing, efforts are made to guarantee that a student is granted due process. Virginia Nordby, Executive Assistant to the President and Director of Affirmative Action at the University of Michigan has noted that even the courts have termed due process "an elusive concept" but suggests that at the very least due process requires: notice of the charge or complaint and the facts which support it; nonprejudicial time intervals; a hearing at which there is an opportunity to answer the charges or explain a position; impartial decision making (1977, p. 85). She also notes that there are additional components which might be added, and these too, can be found in the University of Michigan's procedures. These include the right to confront and question the accuser, the right to call and cross-examine witnesses, representation by legal counsel, a record of the hearing, and a decision based solely on the evidence presented at the hearing.

It is important to note that the process for resolving a grievance ranges from mediation (either on the part of the student, the Ombudsman, or the Referee) to more formal, arbitrated decision made by the Referee, the Panel, or the Board.

During the four years these procedures have been in place a variety of grievances have been handled. Rarely is a grievance confined to a single, simple issue; grievances about grading and evaluation, for example, are often related to claims of "unfair treatment" or to "unfair rules, or procedures." Receiving a low grade may result in a change in student status, which may in turn effect the awarding of financial assistance or result in the termination of a student's degree program. The overwhelming majority of the grievances filed at the Graduate School have been mediated informally by the Referee. Only a few have resulted in an arbitrated decision by the Referee and only four have gone to the Appeals Panel. Of these four, only two have been brought to a full Board hearing.

Functions and Implications

The primary purpose of enacting student appeals procedures is to provide students with adequate, legally based channels for airing perceived injustices or inequities. Administrators fear that students will use these procedures to harass or embarrass faculty or that enacting the procedures will be time consuming and costly. However, it should be clear that these procedures can serve an important administrative function for an institution. As Virginia Nordby has stated: "The main institutional goal in providing students with Grievance Procedures is to give the institution a mechanism for quickly identifying and correcting its own mistakes. Orderly Grievance Procedures also protect trustees and other high officials from the importunings of individual students who feel they have been treated unjustly but have no 'channels' available for complaining. Finally, institutional student Grievance Procedures may forestall judicial interference in the educational operation of the university" (1977, p. 80).

The establishment of student appeals procedures during the last decade raises several important and as yet unanswered questions about the process of dispute settlement in institutions of higher education. Among these issues are: How do different types of grievance procedures affect the outcomes of student appeals? Under what conditions are arbitrative and mediative decisions likely to be made? What part does the nonadversarial relationship between student and faculty play in the resolution of student grievances? What impact have appeals decisions had on university policies and codes of conduct? Answers to these questions may allow university administrators to design appeals procedures which meet the requirements of due process, encourage the internal review of institutional policies and foster constructive conflict resolution.

References

Carnegie Council on Policy Studies in Higher Education. *Fair Practices in Higher Education: Rights and Responsibilities of Students and Their Colleges in a Period of Intensified Competition for Enrollments.* San Francisco: Jossey-Bass, 1979.

Edwards, H. T., and Nordin, V. D. *Higher Education and the Law.* Cambridge, Mass.: Institute for Educational Management, Harvard University, 1979.

El-Khawas, E. "To Assure Fair Practice Toward Students: A Proposed Code for Colleges and Universities." Washington, D.C.: Office of Self-Regulation Initiatives, American Council on Education, 1979.

Nordby, V. "Due Process for Students: Converting Legal Mandates into Workable Institutional Procedures." In J. Peterson (Ed.), *Higher Education and the Law: An Administrator's Overview.* Toledo, Ohio: Center for the Study of Higher Education, University of Toledo, 1977.

Stark, J. *The Many Faces of Educational Consumerism.* Lexington, Mass.: Lexington Books, 1977.

Janelle Shubert is an instructor in the Department of Communication and is the Rackham Graduate School Appeals Referee at the University of Michigan.

Joseph Folger is an assistant professor in the Department of Communication at the University of Michigan. Together, they have been conducting a national survey of four-year college and university procedures for handling student grievances.

Efforts at the University of Massachusetts at Amherst illustrate how academic programs such as legal studies can form the basis for conflict resolution in the local community as well as on campus.

Legal Studies and Mediation

Janet Rifkin
Peter d'Errico
Ethan Katsh

Law, Mediation, and Legal Studies

The study of conflict and its resolution lies at the core of many disciplines, but perhaps none touches as closely on this subject as legal studies, the liberal arts study of law in society. Legal studies examines the form and structure of authority in society and the conflicts that authority is expected to resolve. Legal studies also examines the role of officially sanctioned authority in exacerbating conflict.

Humanistic, liberal arts legal studies differs considerably from its law school counterpart, the professional study of law. While law school builds its curriculum around the needs of a profession, a liberal arts curriculum operates within a broader context: the study of power and conflict within cultural and historical perspectives. As distinct from a pre-law curriculum, legal studies explores legal issues that arise in connection with the design of public policy and the content of public interest research. Legal studies is not limited to the study of adjudication and adversary processes. It takes these as the dominant themes for conflict management in our society and examines their development and relationship to the structure of society. Official systems of dispute resolution are compared with informal systems, such as the family. Methods for dispute resolution in different institutions within society are compared with each other. Literary and artistic portrayals of conflict and resolution are studied for the insights they provide on society and human behavior.

In short, the liberal arts legal studies curriculum uses law as a window on society. Through this window we view the conflicting and reinforcing social tensions out of which legal concepts and institutions arise. Thus, it is no accident that the Legal Studies Program at the University of Massachusetts at Amherst is involved with the study of mediation as a mode of conflict resolution. The curriculum includes material on nonadversary concepts and processes for handling conflict: a course on the legal profession reviews the extent to which lawyers engage in negotiation and bargaining as well as litigation; a course on mental health law examines the shortcomings of adversarial procedures in protecting social and personal interests in this area; a course on Indian law contrasts the adversarial, hierarchical features of Anglo-European culture with the consensual, participatory characteristics of Native American culture.

Legal studies programs examine the origins of the adjudicatory system and the prospects for introducing alternative systems for resolving conflict in society. Mechanisms that are used for resolving disputes in other countries are analyzed. For example, we study the processes for resolving conflict in China, where there is an ancient cultural antipathy to legalism and the state encourages participatory modes of economic and political decision making. Such a study provides an example of the planned intermingling of mediational and adjudicatory processes in a large society. As the reign of law in American society experiences stress, we may be able to draw information from the Chinese experience that could be useful in exploring such issues as: the types of disputes most amenable to mediation processes; the desirability of resolving conflict in an authoritative way so as to create a framework of "precedent"; the extent to which the mediation of social conflict must be coupled with participatory modes of economic decision making; the link between the adjudicatory and mediation processes in which law sets parameters for mediated results. In approaching these issues from within both a theoretical and an empirical framework, the experiences of other cultures are particularly relevant.

The central theme in the Legal Studies Program is that law is public; public in that it is rooted in and has its effect upon the entire society. In presenting a mechanism for conflict resolution, in channeling behavior according to one value system or another, and in sanctioning the distribution of social benefits and burdens, law itself presents a pressing public issue. In light of the manifest centrality of law in life, it is incongruous that historically the study of law has been largely restricted to the would-be professional lawyer. One of the main activities in the Legal Studies Program is to remedy this incongruity, for law is simply too important to be left to lawyers.

The relationship of law to society is examined in all legal studies courses and recurring fundamental questions about the nature of this relationship define the theoretical boundaries of the Legal Studies Program. Perhaps the most basic of these questions is that of the limitations inherent in litigation as the primary form of conflict resolution in this country.

In legal studies courses, litigation and the adversary process are critiqued and analyzed. Law is described as one of several available methods of dispute resolution. An attempt, therefore, is made to understand why other modes of conflict resolution, such as mediation, have been overpowered by the adversary mode.

This important issue led members of the Legal Studies Program to propose the establishment of a dispute resolution center where mediation would be used as an alternative to the adversary process for disputes which take place on the Amherst campus of the University of Massachusetts. The dispute resolution center would also handle some conflicts that are now sent to court and problems generally troublesome to local communities.

From a legal perspective, conflict is seen as a deviation from the rules. From the perspective of mediation, conflict is seen as a necessary and potentially useful human expression that can ultimately lead to positive social change. Legal studies, in examining the operation of power and authority in specific institutions—such as prisons, families, and workplaces—look for the patterns from which conflict occurs and how it is managed productively. Institutions bound closely by rules and direct coercion, such as prisons, have provided significant examples of the use of informal dispute resolution methods as an alternative to rigid legal enforcement. Family disputes, normally arising out of an atmosphere of intense emotional involvement and usually not related to any official set of rules, may sometimes require formal legal processes to achieve resolution. In many workplaces, the most satisfactory method for handling conflict may be participatory procedures that are designed and accepted by the workers. Tension and cross currents will always be present as the parties in conflict wrestle with the task of solving problems equitably within the context of their ongoing relationships.

Mediation is now explicity recognized and promoted as an alternative to adversary legal processes in the resolution of social conflict. Criminal and civil disputes are being diverted from the courts and litigation; neighborhood justice centers, already operational in a number of locations around the country, are demonstrating that a wide variety of social troubles can be resolved through the voluntary and consensual agreement of the persons involved. Perhaps even more noteworthy, these centers provide evidence that mediation can assist in alleviating some of the deep social tensions that underlie situations of open conflict. This evidence demonstrates that mediation is useful in realms of human relations that can never be reached by the courts operating under the rule of law. Rules of law, designed to regulate overt and observable behavior, address the symptoms of social disorder rather than the roots.

The Dispute Resolution Center

The University of Massachusetts at Amherst offers a particularly suitable setting in which to establish a public/academic dispute resolution center. The university is virtually a city in itself, located in an otherwise rural area on the fringe of a major metropolitan population. The university has a student population of approximately 25,000, a faculty of 1,400, and support staff numbering nearly 3,000. Its Department of Public Safety is the largest force of professionally trained police officers in western Massachusetts outside the urban centers of Springfield and Holyoke. As in any community of this size and density, there is a high volume of criminal activity ranging from thefts and petty vandalism to rape and serious assaults. There are also a wide variety of civil disputes, some of which are unique to academic institutions — such as student-faculty conflicts, dormitory problems, fraternity issues, and racial and sexual tensions. Data from the campus police and from other campus agencies indicate a large number and wide range of cases involving university discipline at all levels in the system.

A large portion of the local court's caseload is directly traceable to disputes within the university. More significantly, however, much of the conflict on campus is left unresolved, or is processed through an archaic and dysfunctional student judicial and disciplinary system. For every case that is sent to the district court, there may be as many as two cases that are not litigated, often because they are ill suited to judicial resolution because of evidential or other deficiencies. These unresolved cases reflect serious underlying conflicts that aggravate social tensions at the university.

The potential for mediation at the University of Massachusetts is high. Administrators, staff, faculty, and students strongly support the creation of a mediation mechanism within the university. This support is based on the recognition that mediation could greatly enhance the quality of life on campus by reducing the university's reliance on the formal legal system, which is considered a last resort in the management of conflict. Both the Chancellor and the Dean of Students support the establishment of a mediation center as a new approach for the resolution of conflict on campus.

The dispute resolution center at the University of Massachusetts at Amherst is drawing for its design from the experiences of other mediation projects around the country where the process is being used effectively, particularly in conflict situations where the disputants have a sustained relationship with each other. The Center will provide a mediation mechanism for conflicts that take place on the campus of the university as well as community conflicts that frequently end up in court.

The center's initial caseload will include community- and university-based disputes that are not amenable to judicial resolution; many of these represent social conflicts that could produce criminal conduct if the underlying issues remain unresolved. The center will deal with a broad range of conflicts:

assaultive and disruptive problems in the dormitories; some conflicts between students and faculty; some problems between faculty and administration; some issues between students and the administration; environmental conflicts, such as health and safety issues for workers in on-campus facilities; consumer conflicts; and housing conflicts, among others. The availability of a campus-based mediation service offers the possibility of resolving disputes through a process that is solution oriented rather than punishment oriented.

The center will begin its mediation activities in February 1981. In fall 1980, the Legal Studies Program will offer its second seminar in dispute resolution. The seminar will present the theoretical framework around which mediation and negotiation strategy is designed, and will draw on guest speakers who have practical experience in dispute settlement in a variety of contexts.

During the fall of 1980, the director of the center will work closely with constituent groups within the university and the community at large to develop an understanding of the center's objectives and the role it expects to play within the community and the university. A series of workshops will be conducted to acquaint members of the university and the community with the center and the techniques involved in mediation. An important focus will be residential areas and the university-based social service organizations, such as counseling and health centers, and groups for women and minorities. These organizations are actively involved in providing services to members of the university community, and thus are in an excellent position to provide referrals to the dispute resolution center.

Before the end of the year, twenty to thirty individuals will be selected to be trained as mediators. In January 1981, the month-long training of mediators will take place. It will be conducted by experienced trainers from the Urban Court Mediation Project in Dorchester, Massachusetts. The training will rely heavily on the use of simulation and group participation in role plays that reflect the range of disputes these mediators will be expected to handle. The workshop participants will include faculty, students, staff, and members of the local community, including police and court-related personnel.

Potential mediators will be required to engage in practical work within the center as intake and case follow-up workers. The practical work of intake will acquaint mediator trainees with the operation and management of the center as well as assist the center in the essential pre- and post-mediation work.

During the center's formative stages it must necessarily rely on trainers from outside the university. After the first year, however, training programs will be conducted by the Legal Studies Program. Since Legal Studies currently offers courses in mediation, we expect to be able to rapidly develop the capability to train student, staff, and community members in mediation techniques.

As an integral part of the project, the Legal Studies Program will generate curriculum materials and conduct research on the role of mediation and its relationship with law and society. The Legal Studies Program is well-situated to evaluate the effectiveness of the training process and to adapt training procedures to the specific needs of the university and the community. Since an important aspect of the Legal Studies Program is the study of alternatives to litigation, with an emphasis on nonadversarial models, students in this program are expected to show great interest in the center. The director of the Legal Studies Program has been appointed ombudsman for the university. This provides an excellent opportunity to coordinate the mediation activities with the ombudsman's office.

This new dispute resolution center draws heavily on the skills and experience of individuals in both the academic and public sectors. It provides students, university staff and community people who possess the ability and the commitment, an opportunity to serve as mediators. Mediating conflict, rather than litigating problems or ignoring them, offers the possibility for addressing some of the most basic issues that occur in community and university life. In this way, mediation offers the possibility for making fundamental and positive changes in people's lives.

Janet Rifkin is ombudsman for the University of Massachusetts at Amherst, director of the dispute resolution project, and associate professor of legal studies.

Peter d'Errico and Ethan Katsh are associate professors in the Legal Studies Program, University of Massachusetts at Amherst.

There are ways to change higher education's reactive stance to government regulation.

Taking the Initiative: Alternatives to Government Regulation

Linda Stamato

Just under two decades have passed since higher education enjoyed halcyon days in its relations with a munificent government. Now, the "splendid isolation" of the early 1960s seems far removed indeed. Government-mandated social legislation and the related directives and guidelines from federal agencies define a good part of contemporary academic life: exemptions and immunities no longer set the academy apart from society.

The federal government's role in higher education today reveals programs so numerous, goals so varied, administration so fragmented, and results so uneven that it is doubtful that anyone can grasp the entire picture. The 4000-odd government programs, the $15 billion in annual expenditures, and the accompanying regulatory maze vary in importance among institutions, but in one way or another, all are affected. The terms *accountability, consumer protection, nondiscrimination,* and *affirmative action* take on special significance reflecting the growth of regulation and the response of institutions to the increasingly active (some say intrusive) role of government in the affairs of colleges and universities. Thus the presence of government is one of the most discernible and disturbing features on the contemporary academic scene.

Comment on this development has ranged the full spectrum: there are those who see governmental activity as undermining the necessary independence of institutions, those who believe that governmental action has been constructive for the most part in achieving desirable social and political objectives, and those who believe government has not gone for enough. All, however, are concerned about the potential for future abuses that are likely in a relationship which, given the differences in goals and patterns of operation, is inevitably fraught with tension and conflict. Of particular concern are those characteristics of colleges and universities that some educators see as entitlements to exemption or special treatment when broad social legislation is undertaken because the autonomy, integrity, and traditional character of higher education rests in the balance. Few educators would defend discrimination on the basis of sex or race, argue for unsafe laboratories, advocate buildings that are inaccessible to the handicapped, or question protective legislation in these areas. The issue is not the intent of the legislation but the related directives and guidelines that are said to be excessive, clumsy, costly, contradictory, and counterproductive, and the need of colleges and universities to decide for themselves such matters as academic standards, hiring and promotion policies, criteria for admission, and internal governance practices.

Higher education has an interest in finding better methods to effectuate sound public policy. It is not enough simply to repudiate the concept and practice of federal regulation without offering equivalent means to meet legislatively determined goals. Academic leaders ought to devote some considerable energy and ingenuity to the pursuit of alternatives for meeting those goals with which they agree through a process that respects the integrity and autonomy of the institutions they lead and defend. Otherwise, higher education's commitment to those goals will appear disingenuous. Academe would then not only be unable to restrain the growth of government influence, it would contribute to that growth and the concomitant compromise of its own freedom and integrity.

Origins and Trends of Federal Regulation

In seeking to improve federal regulations, we should recall that these regulations result from laws or executive orders enacted in response to constituent pressure. Chester Finn, formerly of the Brookings Institution, states the case succinctly: "Those constituencies now monitor the performance of the government enforcers with fierce dedication and single-minded enthusiasm. The bureaucrats are not to be blamed, except perhaps for occasional excess or whimsy in interpreting the law. It is the lawmakers who are responsible, but they acted in order to help or appease groups that sought changes. Hence anyone who seeks to mitigate the effects of government regulation on colleges and universities had best recognize at the outset that it is not a struggle between the academy and the bureaucracy, but between parts of the society that want change and parts that resist change" (1978, p. 141).

Finn's reminder serves to emphasize the need to develop methods — particularly self-regulatory mechanisms — that can satisfy constituent interests and minimize the case for government control. Beyond current "command and control" models of regulation that rest primarily on procedural due process or the probability of judicial intervention, more effective and salutary methods deserve trial in satisfying constituent interests. Among several new trends in federal regulation, four are particularly promising in focusing on a societal goal and encouraging those responsible for an enterprise to find the best way to achieve it.

The first of these methods can be best described as a *market-oriented approach,* in that it relies less on prescribing specific requirements than on the economic incentives of the free market to nudge organizations in the direction of the public interest. For example, the Environmental Protection Agency is seeking to regulate the noise level of products by means of this approach, by requiring these levels be noted on product labels.

The second category involves *performance standards.* Instead of delineating precisely how an industry must meet particular goals, broad goals are set forth that leave the means to reach them largely up to industry. Thus the Occupational Safety and Health Administration is using a performance standard approach in dropping some 900 "general industry" regulations that governed, among other items, the dimensions of ladders and fire extinguishers, and in reducing these regulations from 400 to 30 pages, allowing employers simply to certify that they have adequate evacuation plans in case of fire. It has eschewed the use of economic incentives to achieve safe and healthful workplaces in preference to encouraging management and labor to form joint committees to oversee safety and health practices.

The third approach, that of *information disclosure,* rests on the principle that consumers can make intelligent choices if given sufficient facts. It requires manufacturing and service industries to disclose detailed information about their products and services. For instance, the Food and Drug Administration has moved to implement information disclosure methods in requiring drug companies to provide information on the purposes of their products and possible adverse reactions to them in language the public can understand. Similarly, the Federal Trade Commission employed this approach is its voluntary disclosure agreement reached with the cigarette industry in 1971 and in more recent standards for funeral homes, and the Commission is moving in the direction of utilizing this approach in regulating the sale of used cars and home appliances.

Self-regulation forms the fourth category; it involves assisting industry in setting its own voluntary standards — standards, however, that, from the agency's point of view, are enforceable and in the public interest. Thus at the Consumer Product Safety Commission, the standard-setting process for the 10,000 products that fall within its jurisdiction was so time consuming and burdensome that in the five years since its creation, it had managed to issue standards only on matchbooks, swimming pool slides, lawnmowers, and a handful of other items. As a result, the Commission has now abandoned unilateral standard setting and intends to work with industry groups to set voluntary product safety standards. The move to industry self-regulation, according to one of the Commission's members (Statler, 1979), is based on the tremendous amount of talent in industry that can be directed toward developing product standards, the decline in the Commission's suspicion of industry motives, and its more realistic attitude toward its limited resources to deal with the vast range of consumer products.

No doubt these approaches have their limitations for institutions of higher education: Certainly higher education does not fully constitute a free market; performance standards, uniformly and rigidly applied, could have a disastrous effect on diversity, a universally acknowledged value of American higher education; information disclosure cannot protect all prospective students; and self-regulation has not generated great interest among institutions. But these new initiatives, when properly applied, hold considerable promise of conforming to the values of colleges and universities, meeting the needs of students, and satisfying the general public interest. Design and implementation are crucial. Given the variety of techniques available, it is incumbent upon higher education and government to decide upon the most appropriate regulatory methods—appropriate in the sense of what is most likely to achieve the desired outcome and what is the least likely to harm the academic enterprise. According to Derek Bok, "the government has an opportunity to do a much better job of reconciling the interests of higher education with other public concerns by making sounder choices of regulatory techniques" (1980, p. 87). It is not likely to seize that opportunity, however, without the initiative and assistance of higher education.

Self-Regulation and Performance Standards as Strategies for Higher Education

The academic community's interest in affecting government regulation should find expression in efforts to improve the rule-making process so that regulations, arrived at cooperatively, can be effective without eroding institutional autonomy or placing unnecessary burdens on colleges and universities.

Self-regulation merits special consideration in this regard; its distinctive features place it high on the list of alternative regulatory modes for the academy. Jack Peltason, President of the American Council on Education, states the case (1978) "Issues currently being addressed by regulatory efforts could be more effectively resolved by voluntary initiatives within the higher education community to address these problems and identify means of resolving them. Stronger efforts in this regard can help obviate the need for further governmental intervention."

One example of self-regulation already in place is the system for reviewing and monitoring experimental biomedical research involving human subjects. The system, mandated by federal legislation for all institutions receiving Health and Human Services funds, provides for the creation of institutional review boards, whereby each university appoints some fifteen to twenty-five persons from the university and the community at large to review research proposals. The system is one of peer review with public input, not one of government regulation. No federal officials review the research proposals; they simply ensure that universities comply with the law by establishing and maintaining review boards. Such a system preserves both the rights and the autonomy of potential research subjects and the rights of researchers to conduct their investigations in a free and unfettered manner.*

Perhaps no example serves better to illustrate the need for academic initiative in influencing government regulation than the relationship in recent years between the Veterans Administration and American colleges and universities. Educators have charged the VA with challenging the traditional rights of academic institutions to establish and control the content of academic programs and the means by which they are taught. A major bone of contention has been the VA's prescription of the amount of classroom time students have to spend in a course in order to receive government payments. The VA has made its own determinat'on as to what constitutes legitimate full-time courses, for which full-time benefits would be paid.

This dispute eventually came to involve not only the VA and at least two academic institutions—Wayne State University in Michigan and The Evergreen State College in Washington—in court, but also members of Congress and representatives of the Washington-based education associations, notably the American Council on Education. Resolution may finally be in the offing if a recommendation offered by the VA's Advisory Committee on Education and Rehabilitation, a panel composed of veterans, educators and other outside experts, is accepted. It recommends that benefits be paid for nontraditional courses on "the equivalency of the level of effort required from the veteran

---

*The extension of these regulations beyond biomedical studies to all research involving human subjects (thereby embracing the social sciences) has been less than well received by the academic community and, in some cases, has been viewed as "prior restraint" or outright censorship of social scientific and humanistic research. See, for example, Pool, 1979. Nonetheless, Arthur L. Caplan defends the extension of peer review to social scientific inquiry in Caplan, 1979. See also a discussion of the issue in *EPE: 15 Minute Report,* 1979, p. 4.

compared to standard courses"—a performance standard approach. Course credit would be calculated for an entire semester or term rather than on a weekly basis as the regulations have required.

Whatever the outcome, it is clear that this long-standing, costly, and acriminious feud would not have taken place if academic institutions had been involved initially in influencing eligibility policy. Correcting problems of fraud in the use of VA education benefits could have been handled by promulgating regulations with the academic community's participation, or, in other instances, on a self-regulatory basis if self-regulatory practices had been firmly in place. Whether it was intransigence on the part of the VA or unwillingness on the part of some academic institutions to be concerned with the abuse of benefits by others, it is obvious that a sufficient level of cooperation was not present. The imposition of administrative burdens and the restriction of educational opportunities might not have occurred had the VA and these institutions worked together to accomplish the intentions of Congress in improving and reforming the Veterans Education Program.

A recent example of the potential for cooperation between the academy and government concerns the American Association of Collegiate Registrars and Admissions Officers (AACRAO) and the Social Security Administration (SSA). The Administration, having determined that some students who were ineligible for aid, were being paid benefits for months in which they were not actually attending classes, sought the assistance of AACRAO. AACRAO worked out a form and verification procedure that satisfied the SSA; the problem has been virtually eliminated; and the SSA estimates a saving of $30 million in the first year that the procedure has been in effect.

As these examples suggest, the higher education community ought not to continue the battle against government regulations on the grounds that higher education deserves a special exemption from regulation; as Paul Seabury) and others suggest (1979), it ought to draw a different line of defense. Admittedly, precious few unregulated areas remain, but demonstrating a capacity for self-regulation is an important step for academe in making the case for alternatives to "command and control" regulation. Consensual agreements, crafted by academics in cooperation with federal regulators, will more properly reflect the collegial setting and, as such, will address the needs of individuals and agencies in a manner compatible with the values of the academic community.

Campus Initiatives to Avoid Grievances

Higher education needs not only to influence the development of regulations and to participate in the regulation-making process but also to minimize the negative impact of regulations by enhancing the prospect for equitable resolution of complaints that arise in respect to regulations before these complaints reach government agencies and the courts. Presently the enforcement of public goals as expressed in statutes, regulations and legal rulings lies primarily with government agencies and the courts; higher education's role is largely reactive. But in complying with these regulations, whether in the area of alleged discriminatory practices or consumer protection or elsewhere, opportunities exist to develop complaint procedures within the academic community that are far more effective and salutary than procedural models developed by administrative agencies or those that are judicially imposed.

The adjudicative model of resolving complaints, for example, formal court proceedings or in administrative hearings, is not designed to accommodate the vast caseload that presently exists. Thus as of 1975, 126,000 cases were pending before the Equal Employment Opportunity Commission, for example, making the average wait for hearing in an EEOC suit from four to six years. And, it may create more tensions than it resolves. Crystal Lloyd-Campbell, research director of the Sloan Commission on Government and Higher Education, describes the variety and complexity of problems attending the adjudicative approach (1978, p. 3):

> Issues which in reality are complex and indistinct are cast in sharp (and unreal) contrast. Courtroom style places issues in a two-dimensional "we-they" contest and assumes government antidiscrimination enforcement agencies are efficient brokers between protected class groups (minorities, women, handicapped, et al.) on one hand and academia on the other. This assumption may be far from reality. On both sides there is a complex interplay of interests; among the disadvantaged groups as well as academia. A brokerage role for governmental agencies may well be an impossible task given the complexity of the interests and the operational and political constraints which affect academic institutions.
>
> In addition, judicial remedies and agency action presumes bureaucratic leadership is the operative model for academic systems, whereas academia has long valued a system of collegial, overlapping and deliberately diffused responsibility . . .
>
> For individual plaintiffs, particularly academic employment cases, an adversarial model as a means of providing remedial relief is even more unsatisfactory. Admission to the academic "club" is not won in the courtroom. Judicial injunctive remedies which compel employment or tenure ignore the sociology of the collegial departmental structure. Remedies short of compelling employment, such as back pay, may recoup financial loss, but litigiousness is not an attribute which enhances one's reputation in an academic discipline. An individual litigant may win the immediate battle at great emotional and economic cost, only to lose the academic war.

Many decisions, even important ones, will have to be made privately as private agreements, and this fact alone creates the necessity to develop innovative ways to structure, guide, and review private action. Coupled with the need for the academic community to assume more responsibility for itself and its concomitant desire for less direct government regulation, the case is compelling for resolving complaints arising in the application of regulations before government agencies become involved. The intention is to preserve and enhance the autonomy of academic institutions while dealing equitably and efficiently with complaints regarding them. Institutions that can satisfactorily respond to complaints originating on their campuses are in a position to defend self-regulation and make the case for independence. The absence of effective complaint handling burdens the administrative hearing process and the court system even as it invites further governmental intervention. In contrast, ready access to processes offering the possibility of reaching a just settlement expeditiously could prove attractive to complainants, particularly in view of the current lack of prompt redress through administrative agencies and the courts.

Resolution naturally should begin where the complaint arises, such as between a student and a professor, but even acknowledging fairly sophisticated two-party grievance mechanisms on many campuses, many complaints are not resolved at that level. As a result, mediation and other forms of third-party assistance are needed. As social inventions, they have transformed the method of engagement from destructive combat to constructive problem solving without, in so doing, abridging the rights of individuals to seek redress of grievances by adjudication if they remain dissatisfied.

Third-party intervention techniques, including mediation, have been used successfully as an alternative and as an adjunct to the court system in many jurisdictions, particularly in dealing with petty crimes and juvenile matters, and in some instances courts have turned to third parties to help resolve conflicts, particularly those relating to school desegregation. Mediation is a viable alternative because it encourages voluntary agreement on solutions that allow each side to preserve the points it considers essential, rather than imposing win/lose settlements, such as result from legal suits and other adjudicative action. Mediation also provides a forum in which the full range of issues in a dispute may be explored — issues that are often excluded from the courtroom process. Drawn up by the very people who must live with them, the resulting solutions are more likely to reflect their needs than imposed decisions and, as such, they promote a better ongoing relationship between the parties, who often must continue to deal with each other once the conflict has been resolved.

In academe, mediation is beginning to attract attention as a serious effort to avoid excessively formalistic methods, to minimize protracted conflict, and to replace adversarial methods of one kind or another, as illustrated by the mediation efforts of the American Association of University Professors, the American Association of University Administrators, and the Center for Mediation in Higher Education, described earlier in this volume. Several government initiatives can be cited as well: The Office of Civil Rights has an early complaint resolution process and the Equal Employment Opportunity Commission (EEOC) has a rapid charge process, both of which involve a mediation step. And last year, the Department of Health, Education, and Welfare established a mediation component in its process for handling age discrimination complaints.

This is not to say, however, that mediation has no limitations. The underside of its primary asset, its flexibility, can be perceived as mere inconsistency; resolution of similar complaints may vary widely; and some complainants will likely accept less than their full legal entitlements. But as Linda Singer has said (1978, p. 18),"Such compromise may be a price willingly paid for a speedy settlement of a complainant's problem. In mediating complaints, the primary goal is a settlement satisfactory to both parties, not the evolution of a body of law."

The self-interest of complainants, together with the skill and guidance of mediators, will have to be relied upon to produce solutions that vindicate the intentions of the goal at hand, whether it is nondiscrimination, or relates to a health and safety issue.

Both formal agency investigation and enforcement proceedings and litigation through the courts can and do provide authoritative interpretations of legislative mandates concerning, for example, the precise boundaries of the statutory prohibitions against discrimination based upon sex, age or handicap. The existence of more precise standards will increase the likelihood of successful mediation in the future.

The salient point is that mediation is a desirable alternative for those who wish to avoid the prospect of a costly, time-consuming and uncertain agency or judicial proceeding. Mediation is not so much a substitute for more formal enforcement processes as it is a complement to them that specifically allows a redirection of resources to the more intractable disputes — usually those that will assist in interpreting and applying statutes.

Present legal protections not only remain available in situations where the mediation process fails, but they serve to provide an incentive to academic institutions to continue to act upon their commitments in effective ways. The expectation is, of course, that the mediation process would defer the call on formal legal machinery from an earlier to a later stage in the dispute resolution process with the purpose of developing effective institutional initiatives that will obviate the need for administrative regulatory review or recourse to the courts.

As Carl Kaysen points out, however, "emphasis on institutional initiatives and the creation of a series of informal steps in dispute resolution before the application of formal, legally binding proceedings are not typical in the federally regulated sectors of industry" (1979, p. 50). And, the successful operation of negotiating and mediating procedures would also involve a change in the role of the courts as regulatory bodies:

Because aggrieved individuals, especially in situations involving allegations of forbidden discrimination . . . seek direct redress in the courts, rather than relying on the agencies of the executive branch to vindicate their rights, the courts have become major actors on the educational scene . . . . The formality of court procedures, their expense, the inevitable intensification of conflictual elements that the adversary process entails, all warrant the search for ways to diminish the role of the courts.

The strategy of such a change must focus on postponement, on making litigation the last rather than the first step in the process of dispute settlement, since the constitutional role of the courts as ultimate arbiters of the legal rights of individuals remains. Here again, analogy to the traditional forms of industrial regulation may be apposite. Appeals to the courts in those areas can take place only after administrative remedies have been exhausted. In the context of higher education, these administrative remedies would have to be understood as giving a central place to the informal procedures (pp. 50–51).

Notwithstanding the cost and dissatisfaction with the courts and administrative agencies, they remain the primary forums for conflict resolution. Alternative, nonadversarial styles involving third-party assistance, for example, have rarely been utilized for resolving antidiscrimination or other conflicts on American campuses.

Mediation and the Grievance Process

The creation of effective grievance machinery in higher education requires the existence of some individual or agency, either on campus or serving several campuses, to which aggrieved individuals or groups could turn when other steps prior to agency investigation or litigation fall short of providing satisfactory resolution of complaints.

Effective conflict resolution can lead not only to improved relationships on campus, to more individual satisfaction and, thus, to less recourse to formal and more costly adjudicative mechanisms, but can contribute in salutary fashion to campus governance by highlighting areas in organizations, function and personnel where change is required.

Among campus mediation efforts that attempt to obviate the necessity for administrative agency review or recourse to the courts by providing an informal means to resolve complaints, the Massachusetts Institute of Technology has created an inhouse mediation and obmudsman service applicable to all employees of the institution, students, prospective students, and even outsiders who believe they have a claim on the Institute's resources. The service is attached to the offices of the President and the Chancellor. According to Mary

P. Rowe, its director, the ambience of MIT invites cooperative problem-solving approaches. The result is "reduced total costs for dissatisfaction in terms of law-suits, government interference, absenteeism, turnover, theft and sabotage," although, Rowe says, "our good fortune in these areas is hard to assess, hard to attribute to causes and, of course, very vulnerable to change" (1979).

At Northeastern University, a grievance procedure, recommended by the Faculty Senate and ratified by the University's non-unionized faculty, was adopted by the Board of Trustees in 1973. Besides including standard action-able items in the definition of a grievance, it allows grievances to be pursued whenever a faculty member feels he or she has otherwise been treated unfairly or inequitably. The last step in the procedure provides for a final and binding decision by a professional arbitrator who is affiliated with another university, but in addition to fairly typical steps, it provides for mediation. An ad hoc mediation Committee composed of three faculty members appointed by the Faculty Senate provides faculty support and guidance in helping to resolve the grievance, attends the various hearings at each step of the proceeding, and lends its good offices in suggesting solutions to the conflict (Herman, 1976).

At the University of Pennsylvania, an Office of Ombudsman has since 1971 provided service to all members of the university community who have a grievance or who are involved in a dispute with which they would like assistance. The service is offered on a strictly confidential basis, free of charge and, as the University directory states, "in the hope that its availability will further the Uni-versity's efforts to function as a human institution." A faculty member, on released time, performs the duties of ombudsman on a part-time basis. A full-time administrator, with the title of Assistant Ombudsman, completes the staff. The principal functions of the office are to help protect individual rights and to promote better channels of communication. Those consulting the office — at a rate of approximate 375 annually — have problems relating to academic mat-ters, nonreappointment and tenure, salary, housing, fees, parking, and so forth. Not only has the office contributed to resolution of a myriad of such problems, its efforts have led to systemic reform. Recurring problems in the early years now appear rarely, "primarily because University officials have modified a great many rules in response to patterns of repeated complaints" (Freedman, 1976).

As indicated in the preceding chapter, the University of Massachusetts at Amherst is considering establishing a Dispute Resolution Center that will combine three interwoven components: one unit to offer mediation services to cases that would normally be processed through the District Court; another to provide for mediation of conflicts that emerge from academic dispute mecha-nisms within the University; and, a third, consisting of a clinical and academic teaching program, to train mediators to work in the first two components and to provide research and curricula for the teaching and study of conflict and con-flict resolution in general. The combination of these units would make this Cen-ter unique in the United States.

Future Possibilities

Most present academic grievance procedures, designed primarily to protect faculty from arbitrary and capricious acts of administrators, are not able to promote cooperative problem solving for students, administrators, faculty, and others who believe their governmentally protected rights are denied them. Academic institutions need to develop new self-directed methods of resolving such conflict. Building a mediation component into expanded grievance procedures is one obvious solution that can take several forms. Following the final step of the grievance procedure, for example, mediation could be invoked by voluntary agreement of the parties, or it could be a mandatory step for a prescribed period of time prior to this final step. Drawing upon the traditional voluntarism of the academic community, potential mediators can be attracted from faculty and staff ranks, receive training, and be offered released time or other incentives to function as mediators. As the cases of MIT and the University of Pennsylvania illustrate, an ombudsman/mediation office can be created for the purpose of handling a wide range of disputes.

On a regional basis, colleges and universities could contribute to a fund to support the services of mediators for their several campuses. Disputants could choose from among a panel of mediators the person or persons they wish to have assist them. Or, in states having dispute resolution agencies for public and private sector labor relations, a cooperative arrangement might be considered.

Should mediation fail, the complaint could of course proceed through traditional, established mechanisms — either administrative agencies or the courts. But there are other possibilities here, too. Special expert tribunals might be established to hear cases. By agreement of the parties, the decision of the tribunal would terminate the dispute. Such tribunals ought to be exclusively composed of individuals who are qualified and experienced in academic matters, such as current or retired college administrators, faculty members, trustees, union leaders, and education association staff. These individuals would have a greater appreciation of the dimensions of academic disputes than would federal agency hearing officers, members of the judiciary, or arbitrators having principally labor-management experience in the industrial sector. Panels of such individuals could be established under the aegis of an education association, such as the American Council on Education, or of a regional body. Parties to a dispute could receive a list of the panel members, select acceptable arbitrators for the tribunal, and agree to accept its judgment as binding. Just decisions, arrived at expeditiously and at low cost, can emerge from such a process, as we know from the distinguished record of the labor-management community. And the process of reviewing a substantial number of such cases might develop a uniform and reliable body of precedents. Tailored to the special needs and circumstances of academe, such arbitration could be a satisfactory recourse short of administrative agency or judicial review when mediation fails to bring about a solution.

A range of formal and informal approaches are thus possible that would attract and satisfy complainants and allow private, flexible and cooperative resolution of differences. Structural or other barriers may make it harder for some institutions than others to establish such dispute resolution programs, but the need for them is increasing, given the present circumstances of the academy and government regulation. The traditional ethos of colleges and universities as academic communities is giving way to a highly structured and legalistic climate governed by a web of laws and regulations. The presence of government agencies and the judiciary is ever more visible; tension and conflict persist and divide; and disputes are settled not on campus but by administrative agencies or in court. The frequency and variety of lawsuits and administrative agency proceedings have educational implications for higher education even beyond their economic and social costs.

In the future, higher education institutions must press on several fronts to avoid further outside control of academic affairs: They should help devise methods other than regulation to achieve public policy goals. They should participate in the policy formulation and rule-making process of government so that regulations with which colleges and universities must comply are not unduly costly and do not jeopardize their integrity and autonomy. Pressing for government acceptance of voluntary, self-regulatory initiatives is as important as establishing their validity. And institutions should develop the case for self-regulation by implementing procedures that can satisfactorily resolve conflicts.

Increased self-regulation seems the most promising means to bridge the present gap between government requirements and campus compliance, since society is not likely to restore the exemptions and immunities of the past. Satisfying goals of value to society and, in particular, providing equity to individuals, can be accomplished through voluntary efforts that do not threaten the academic enterprise; indeed, such efforts, well conceived and executed, can preserve and enhance the autonomy, the integrity and even the standing of the academy.

References

Bok, D. C. "The Federal Government and the University." *The Public Interest,* 1980, *58,* 80–101.

Caplan, A. L. "H.E.W.'s Painless Way to Review Human Research." *New York Times,* December 27, 1979.

Clark, T. B. "New Approaches to Regulatory Reform—Letting the Market Do the Job." *National Journal,* 1979, *32,* 1316–1322.

Clark, T. B. "Discrimination Suits: A Unique Settlement." *Educational Record,* Summer 1977, pp. 233–249.

Edwards, H. "Arbitration of Employment Discrimination Cases: A Proposal for Employer and Union Representatives." *Labor Law Journal,* 1971, *27* (5), 265–277.

EPE: 15 Minute Report. December 1979.

Finn, C. E., Jr. *Scholars, Dollars, and Bureaucrats.* Washington, D.C.: The Brookings Institution, 1978.

Freedman, J. O. "What Purpose Does an Ombudsman Serve?" *Almanac,* University of Pennsylvania, May 11, 1976.

Herman, S. "Faculty Grievance Procedures in a Non-Union Context." *Collective Bargaining in Higher Education,* Proceedings, April 1976, pp. 28–35.

Kaysen, C. "The Growing Power of Government." In C. Walton and F. Bolman, (Eds.), *Disorders in Higher Education.* Englewood Cliffs: Prentice-Hall, 1979.

Lloyd-Campbell, C. C. "A Modest Proposal on Conflict: Academia and Alternatives, A Proposed Experiment in Alternative Dispute Resolution Mechanisms." Discussion paper for the Sloan Commission on Government and Higher Education, June 1978.

Peltason, J. "ACE Leads Effort on Self-Regulation," Council on Post-Secondary Education *Newsletter,* Summer, 1978, *3* (4).

Pool, I. D. S. "Prior Restraint." *New York Times,* December 16, 1979.

Rowe, M. P. Assistant to the President and Chancellor, Massachusetts Institute of Technology, conversation with director of the Center for Mediation in Higher Education, New York, May 1979.

Seabury, P. (Ed.). *Bureaucrats and Brainpower: Government Regulation of Universities.* Berkeley, Calif.: Institute for Contemporary Studies, 1979.

Singer, L. "The Use of Mediation in Enforcing the Age Discrimination Act of 1975." Unpublished memorandum, to F. P. Libassi, former General Counsel, H.E.W., November 15, 1978.

Statler, S. "Interview with Investor Responsibility Research Center, Inc." *News for Investors,* 1979, *6* (11), 227–228.

Linda Stamato, a consultant to the Center for Mediation in Higher Education, also has worked in private sector labor relations, at the corporate and dispute resolution levels. Formerly a member of the Commission on Higher Education of the Middle States Association of Colleges and Schools, she is currently a member of the Board of Governors of Rutgers University.

Insights from the behavioral sciences suggest improvements in the academic bargaining process.

Constructive Conflict in Academic Bargaining

Robert Birnbaum

Collective bargaining is a process of shared authority which is used in some institutions to manage conflict which at least one of the parties does not believe can be resolved through more traditional academic structures. The identification of academic bargaining as a form of conflict management does not necessarily suggest its outcomes, however, and indeed conflict can take one of two quite different directions. Conflict can be constructive solving of the problems of the participants and leaving each satisfied with the outcome and with the feeling of having gained as a result. Conflict can also be destructive, resulting in dissatisfaction by both parties and the feeling that each has lost as a consequence (Duetsch, 1969). A specific characteristic of destructive conflict is its tendency to escalate, to increase in size and intensity, to become independent of the processes which caused the initial conflict, and to increasingly rely upon the use of power, coercion, and deception.

Academic bargaining researchers have for the most part viewed the bargaining process from administrative, political, institutional, or legal perspectives, and their work has been extraordinarily useful in helping us to understand

Portions of this chapter are adapted from Birnbaum, R. *Creative Academic Bargaining: Managing Conflict in the Unionized College and University.* New York: Teachers College Press, 1980.

and to a limited extent direct the growth of this relatively recent phenomenon. Overlooked in this early flurry of research and writing, however, has been the fact that academic bargaining can also be usefully viewed as an example of intergroup conflict which, although occurring within certain legal limits and ritualized formats, can engender the same behavioral characteristics seen in other groups in conflict. This chapter briefly explores three basic ideas related to this fact: first, that an understanding of intergroup conflict can be useful in understanding why people behave as they do at the bargaining table; second, it is possible to analyze the accepted structures and processes of academic bargaining to determine if they are likely to support constructive or destructive outcomes; and third, that it is possible to design new orientations and bargaining structures which can help parties use academic bargaining more creatively than they now do.

Competition, Compromise, and Collaboration in Collective Bargaining

The orientation which a group brings to bargaining depends upon: (1) the degree to which it is committed to satisfying its own concerns, and (2) the extent to which it is concerned about the expressed interests of the other group and willing to help them achieve their goals (Thomas, 1976). The orientation which we call *competition* exists when a group wishes to achieve its own goals and has no concern for the interests of the other group at all. This combination of assertiveness and uncooperativeness leads to win-lose bargaining in which the gains of one group are seen to come at the expense of the other. Competition is probably seen by many if not most participants as the natural mode of bargaining, and through predictable intergroup processes which shall be briefly mentioned shortly, it moves the parties almost inexorably towards destructive conflict.

When groups of equal power are involved in competitive conflict the result is often a compromise, a lose-lose orientation to conflict. While competition can lead to one group achieving its goals, compromise ensures that neither party has its interests fully met. There are occasions when compromise is the best outcome that the parties can achieve, particularly when they are bargaining over the allocation of a limited resource. In many cases, however, parties compromise because they are unaware of the creative potential of a situation, because they do not have the problem-solving skills to exploit it, or, as is often the case in collective bargaining, they find themselves in a situation in which compromise is expected by definition and is socially acceptable.

Competition and compromise are not the only available orientations towards conflict, however. When a group combines strong concern for its own interests with an equally strong concern for seeing that the needs of the other group are also met, a collaborative relationship can develop in which the parties search for integrative solutions meeting both of their needs. This requires a problem-solving approach, because such solutions often must be invented by the parties through their joint activities. The collaborative orientation can result in win-win situations, since each party is able to satisfy its needs while at the same time the relationship between them is strengthened and supportive of further cooperative activities. The outcome is constructive conflict.

The thesis of this chapter is that neither compromise nor competition is a constructive means of managing conflict in academic bargaining, and that groups can more fully achieve their own goals not by defeating other groups or "splitting the difference" with them, but by working together towards mutually acceptable solutions. Opportunities for such collaborative approaches should be available in academic bargaining to an even greater extent than in any other collective bargaining setting. Fully realizing these opportunities is, in my judgment, a critical goal if academic bargaining is to serve as a structure for strengthening, rather than dividing, the unionized college or university.

However, if we wish to make bargaining the constructive force for institutional development which it can be, it will be necessary to significantly change its form in some fundamental way. Some of the reasons for this will be found in the nature of conflict between groups in competition.

Competing groups behave in remarkably similar ways, whether they consist of boys engaged in "color war" competition at summer camp, union and management negotiators at the bargaining table, or diplomats who believe each other's interests to be incompatible. Indeed, the dynamics of intergroup conflict can be created in the laboratory by forming groups of individuals who have had no previous contact with one another. On the basis both of these experimental situations and the observations and studies of groups in other competitive settings, a number of generalizations related to academic bargaining can be made.

1. It is possible to create competitive groups merely by placing them in a situation identified as competitive. Academic bargaining is just such a situation.

2. Perceiving a situation as competitive distorts the judgment of group members so that they are likely to overestimate the quality of their solution to a problem, and underestimate that of the opponent. Academic bargainers are likely to think more highly of their own demands than those of the other side, regardless of actual merit.

3. Once a group creates a solution to a problem, it becomes committed to it and is literally unable to understand the elements of alternative solutions. Academic bargainers are likely not to really understand each other's positions, or to accurately assess the importance which the other side attaches to each of its demands.

4. Opportunities to gain further information about an opponent's solutions will be used to attack and belittle the opponent, rather than to study the proposal. The academic bargaining conference will often

be used as a forum for justifying one's own position, and making sarcastic remarks about the position of the other team, rather than trying to understand different perspectives.

5. Stereotypes of the "other side" develop, leading to what has been called (Frank, 1968) the *enemy image*. The image, once established, is maintained and reinforced through restricting communication, selective filtering, and interpretation of the evidence to fit the image.

6. The stress of competitive interaction, often increased by the use of deadlines and threats, distorts the way the parties see the situation, leading to "cognitive and behavioral rigidity, a tendency to react quickly and violently, underestimation of an opponent's capacity for retaliation, interpretation of a conciliatory move on the part of an opponent as a trick or a sign of weakness, a lowered tolerance for ambiguity, and a tendency, on the part of the decision makers, to interpret messages that reinforce their preconceived view of a crisis" (Druckman, 1971, p. 532–533).

These processes of cognitive distortion, stereotyping, premature commitment to alternatives, and inability to understand the position of the opponents, can quickly develop in an academic bargaining situation predefined as competitive, in which the parties may have already attacked each other before bargaining in a representational election, and in which inexperienced parties come to the table without a full understanding of the bargaining process. They tend to lead to destructive conflict in which either one party tries to subdue the other by virtue of superior power, or a compromise is arranged in which both parties lose. Opportunities for creative and collaborative interaction are foregone, and both parties lie in wait for "next time."

Problems of Traditional Academic Bargaining

If these are the natural consequences of groups in conflict, to what extent are they modified by the structures, expectations, and common practices which we have developed in academic bargaining? Does the bargaining relationship change ordinary group interaction so that communication between faculty and administration is enhanced and clarified rather than diminished and muddied, so that levels of trust are increased rather than reduced, and so that collaborative orientations and behaviors replace competitive and destructive ones? To the contrary, I would argue that for the most part our current structures almost appear designed to support a competitive orientation, as do the instructions which bargainers receive from many of us writing in the field. A complete analysis of the effect of accepted structure upon the course of academic bargaining is presented elsewhere (Birnbaum, in press) and is too involved to be given more than brief attention here. Three specific examples should clarify the concept, however.

First, we know that destructive intergroup conflict increases as groups become more uniform internally and more different from each other, and that the potential for destructive conflict decreases as groups are divided by cross-cutting subgroups and have overlapping members. Academic bargaining increases the possibility of destructive conflict by "clarifying" and differentiating the previous fuzzy and overlapping roles of faculty and administration, labelling each separate from the other and having conflicting interests, and requiring each group to present a united front at the bargaining table.

Second, since creative solutions are never obvious ones (if they were, difficult problems would not be difficult), finding answers that meet the needs of both parties requires intensive collaborative activity during which members of both groups can tentatively explore numbers of alternatives. In contrast, academic bargaining proceeds by having each group consider its problems separately, unaware of the needs and interests of the other. Indeed, what we in bargaining call "demands" or "counter offers" are really unilateral solutions to problems. Since they are prepared separately by each side, they tend to be adopted prematurely without full consideration of alternatives. Once each side becomes committed to its own solution it becomes virtually impossible to consider creative alternatives which might not have occurred to either one, and which in fact may be superior for each party than the one they themselves constructed.

As a final example, creative and collaborative bargaining requires the parties to be aware of the interests and values of the other. An orientation towards helping the other party achieve their goals can only be satisfied if those goals are known. Bargaining, on the other hand, relies to a great extent on misdirection, and the limiting of communication. Bargainers are urged to fight for issues they don't care about, to withhold from the opponent an indication of the priorities which are held for different items, and to limit communications at the table to the chief negotiator so that one's real intentions are not inadvertently disclosed.

Each of these three examples, and many others that could be cited, immediately focuses attention upon the competitive aspects of the process, and facilitates the movement toward destructive conflict.

If this analysis is correct, it suggests that academic bargaining as now practiced can have highly unfortunate consequences for institutions utilizing it as a means of managing conflict. Some have suggested that in fact the structures of bargaining are so inimical to the academic process that it should be prohibited, or at least limited in scope so that its impact upon organizational functioning can be minimized. This position, in my judgment has two major weaknesses. First, academic bargaining serves powerful organizational, professional and institutional needs. Merely removing the bargaining relationship will not solve the problems that initially led to bargaining in the first instance, and can in fact increase destructive conflict by removing a channel through which some of these issues can be articulated. The truth of this assertion will be sorely tested in the post-Yeshiva years ahead. Second, through equalizing power and facilitating direct confrontation of the issues, academic bargaining offers an exciting opportunity for creative and constructive approaches to conflict which may not be present without it in many academic institutions.

Academic bargaining can thus be either an extremely useful mechanism for institutional change, or a devastating structure for destructive conflict. The search for alternatives to destructive orientations to academic bargaining, and for processes through which bargaining can be used to support creative problem solving and appropriate levels of faculty involvement in institutional governance is thus a critical need.

In an exciting book about industrial bargaining written fifteen years ago James Healy wrote: "It is easy to say that the parties should bargain imaginatively and exhort them to take advantage of the freedom which collective bargaining can provide if used 'correctly' or imaginatively. However, it is much more difficult to know how to start such an approach. Old prejudices and fears on both sides of the table must be overcome, and in most cases a fundamental change of attitude is required on the part of both parties . . . . Perhaps more widespread is the frustration of being trapped by the traditional methods of bargaining. The parties may desire a more sensible and rational approach to their problems bu do not know where to start, how to proceed or what the eventual outcome might be" (p. 42).

Just as the behavioral sciences can offer insights into the causes of destructive conflict, so they can suggest ways in which the bargaining relationship may be changed. Some of these changes can be tactical in nature, that is, they can be accomplished within present bargaining structures and would have the effect of decreasing the probability of destructive relationships. For example, suggestions to include department chairmen in the unit, to avoid prebargaining strategy, to recognize the union without a representational election (if possible), to avoid use of external negotiators, and to bargain over specific issues rather than matters of principle, are all grounded in behavioral science theory. Each of them and many others like them which are conceptually based, can be helpful in reducing the natural tendency of academic bargaining to move towards destructive conflict. But each by itself cannot really lead to creative bargaining because they all assume that the bargaining relationships and structures remain essentially the same. If we are to develop new bargaining relations more supportive of academic goals and values, we must consider changing the basic strategies and structures within which the parties interact, and not merely the tactics which each brings to the table.

New Approaches to Academic Bargaining

I believe that there are three basic strategic approaches to creative academic bargaining. First, if creative bargaining should be based on problem solving rather than competition, we must alter existing processes to increase their problem-solving potential. Second, if two parties have difficulty regulating conflict, third parties can be used to help them constructively manage it. And third, if the structure of bargaining itself poses a major obstacle, then it can be changed. Since it is not possible in this paper to fully describe each approach in detail, it might be useful here to give an example of just one alternative within each of the three approaches and to briefly mention the conceptual orientations that support it.

Focusing on Problem Solving. The first basic strategy consists of determining the specific aspects of a bargaining relationship that inhibit problem solving and then having the bargainers agree to change them. Many critical elements related to effective problem solving are under the mutual control of the parties in academic bargaining, but usually remain unexamined because they incorrectly assume that they cannot be altered.

One specific barrier to problem solving, and a solution based upon changing bargaining processes, concerns the general acceptance of the notion that once a contract has been agreed to, bargaining should not be done again for a stated term. This approach is consistent with competitive, win-lose bargaining in which the final agreement codifies the power relationship between the parties at the time it was completed, therefore making it always to the disadvantage of one of the parties to change. But for parties committed to the development of more cooperative and collaborative strategies, it would appear more sensible to deal with problems as they emerge, rather than permit them to fester until the arbitrary date upon which contract renegotiations are to begin. One way to permit this is to conceive of bargaining as an ongoing, rather than a periodical process. Acceptance of this concept of *continuous bargaining* might begin with the agreement of both sides to study an issue in the contract which now was considered troublesome by either one of the parties. If agreement on a change could be reached, the revised wording could be inserted at any time into the contract. Initially the parties might wish to limit the number of items for which this could be done. But if the parties found the process agreeable, and developed experience in using it, it is possible to conceive of a situation in which, except for salaries and fringe benefits, "contracts" would not have termination dates. A policy once established through the bargaining process would remain in force until either party wished to have it changed and initiated bargaining concerning it. Done in this manner, each provision could be dealt with as a specific problem and evaluated on its merits, rather than viewed as a potential trade-off for other items under discussion. Parties would be more likely to experiment with new ideas and innovative approaches to problems as well, knowing that if their agreement turned out to have unanticipated consequences, study and possible change could occur at any time.

Using Third Parties. The second basic strategy leading to more constructive bargaining is the use of third parties in the bargaining process. Behavioral scientists have identified a number of constructive functions which third parties can perform in intergroup conflict situations (Deutsch, 1973). Unfortunately, the traditions of collective bargaining support the notion that the best bargains are those arrived at by the two parties without the assistance of neutrals in any form. For that reason, their use in bargaining has for the most part been restricted to involvement at impasse, the point at which the parties have exhausted most of the flexibility in the bargaining situation, and at which a third party can be least effective in supporting creative bargaining approaches.

Rather than consider third parties solely as an alternative at impasse, creative academic bargaining can make use of third parties at various stages in the bargaining process including before bargaining commences, while bargaining is continuing, and even after bargaining has been concluded. For example, one prebargaining approach involved the use of third parties to conduct workshops at which the teams can develop better communications and more accurate understandings about each other (Blake, Mouton, and Sloma, 1965). Destructive conflict caused by intergroup competition leads to misunderstandings of the other's positions, and distortions in their communications systems which perpetuate and intensify the conflict. Parties may develop images of the other which are resistant to change and which make it difficult for them to engage in collaborative activities. In an intergroup conflict workshop which occurs before bargaining starts, third party neutrals work with both bargaining teams to help them to more accurately assess the goals and perceptions of the other, and to achieve a better understanding of the effects of their own behaviors upon those of the other side. The process is based on the theory that the image each group has of the other can be altered through controlled confrontation, and that changes in communication and perceptions will enable the parties to increase levels of trust, identify more clearly the real issues between them, and move toward a more constructive bargaining relationship with greater emphasis upon problem solving. In the two-day sessions required for this activity, third-party neutrals can help each party to develop its images of itself and that of the other group, share these images between groups, and explore the reasons for the discrepancies which exist between the images each group has of itself and the other. These new perceptions constructively alter group interactions when bargaining subsequently begins.

Changing the Bargaining Structure. The third major strategy of creative bargaining is to change the bargaining structure so that the development of collaborative bargaining relationships on some areas is not inhibited by the need to use competitive approaches in others. To understand the conceptual orientation of this approach it is necessary to consider the fact that competitive bargaining is effective in situations in which what one side wins the other loses (as for example in bargaining over salaries), while collaborating bargaining is effective in dealing with situations in which it is possible for both parties working together to win more than either can by competing. Unfortunately, the harsh, secretive, and combative approach of competitive, or distributive bargaining tends to overwhelm the open, trusting, and collaborative problem-solving orientation necessary for integrative bargaining. Because of the need for negotiators to adopt consistent bargaining styles, interactions developed during bargaining for money are likely to interfere with attempts to problem solve on other matters. One solution to this problem is to separate the two kinds of decision processes as much as possible by changing the structure of bargaining itself, by having different people do each, by placing the items on different agendas, by dealing with the items at different times, by establishing ground rules of separation, or by separating issues spatially (Walton and McKersie, 1965).

One common structural way of achieving such separation, although it is usually not referred to or considered in behavioral terms, is through the concept of dual governance. A less utilized alternative is the establishment of joint committees. These committees are groups established by the two bargaining parties charges with the responsibility for investigating one or more specific problem and making recommendations back to the full group. Occasionally such committees may have their agreements inserted directly into the contract. Participants may include members of the bargaining team, persons not on the bargaining team, and occasionally third-party neutrals. The study team meets away from the bargaining table, and engages in problem-solving approaches which are difficult to sustain in the traditional bargaining environment. Study committees make use of many of the devices found through behavioral science research to be effective in problem-solving, integrative bargaining approaches. It makes participants problem centered rather than solution oriented, jointly collects facts shared by all members, forms cross-cutting groups (which reduce destructive conflict), increases consensus needed for effective problem solving, and, by functioning outside the traditional bargaining process, is less affected by stereotypes, group loyalties and a reluctance to agree to proposals presented by the other side. Although some experienced academic bargainers have warned against the use of study committees, I believe they offer an extremely helpful alternative approach to parties interested in bargaining more creatively.

Potential of New Approaches to Bargaining

These brief suggestions indicate that there are a number of ways in which the parties to academic bargaining can significantly alter their relationships to promote constructive and creative outcomes of conflict. Through increasing the problem-solving potential of their bargaining, utilizing third-party interventions to change the bargaining process, or altering the bargaining structure, it is possible to create new models of bargaining which meet the unique needs of the academic enterprise. Three things about the use of these new orientations should be mentioned. First, each is consistent with traditional academic norms, and thus supports the acceptance and integration of bargaining into institutional life with minimal organizational disruption.

Second, these suggestions for new bargaining orientations arise from the felt need to construct bargaining models supported by the findings of behavioral science which are more consistent with the needs of the academic world than the so-called industrial model. It is therefore ironic that each of them has been tried and found to be either highly successful or extremely promising in industrial bargaining contexts. Healy (1965) has reported a number of situations in which variants of continuous bargaining were in use fifteen years ago; pre-bargaining third-party interventions are the programmatic focus of the new Federal Mediation and Conciliation Service (FMCS) program of relations by objectives which have been used in major industrial bargaining disputes (Popular, 1977), and the use of joint study committees has a long history going back to the Armour Automation Committee and the Human Relations Committee in Basic Steel, and continuing to this day (FMCS, 1978).

Finally, these new orientations, including the specific alternatives briefly described here as well as many others which can easily be constructed based upon existing knowledge and experience in diplomacy, industrial relations, and similar applied fields, may have less risk associated with them than the consequences of traditional academic bargaining. True, they are much different from the behaviors and activities commonly supposed to represent academic bargaining. For the most part, they are untried in institutions of higher education. It should be remembered, however, that the adoption of collective bargaining during these early years is itself a risk; its eventual outcomes are far from certain, and its effect upon the future course of higher education and the relationship of faculties to their institutions and their profession can at this time only be the subject of speculation. Yet experience with bargaining in other contexts suggests that, at least in some situations, institutions which fail to understand the powerful dynamics for spiralling conflict inherent in the ordinary structure and processes of bargaining, and to take steps to control them, may find the bonds between faculty and administration disrupted or conceivably destroyed. If this happens, the institution may have lost a good measure of the values that constitute its essence and make it a distinctive agency of society. The risk may be great, but the risks of not acting may be greater.

Bargaining can be a powerful force for creative conflict in the unionized college or university. To utilize it fully, however, it will take much more attention than we have given until now to changing it to better support the needs of the academic world.

References

Birnbaum, R. *Creative Academic Bargaining: Managing Conflict in the Unionized College and University.* New York: Teachers College Press, in press.

Blake, R. R., Mouton, J. S., and Sloma, R. L. "The Union-Management Intergroup Laboratory: Strategy for Resolving Intergroup Conflict." *Journal of Applied Behavorial Science,* 1965, *1,* 25-27.

Deutsch, M. "Conflicts: Productive and Destructive." *Journal of Social Issues,* 1969, *25,* 7-41.

Deutsch, M. *The Resolution of Conflict: Constructive and Destructive Process.* New Haven, Conn.: Yale University Press, 1973.

Druckman, D. "The Influence of the Situation in Interparty Conflict." *Journal of Conflict Resolution,* 1971, *15,* 523–555.

Federal Mediation and Conciliation Service. *Thirty-First Annual Report: Fiscal Year 1978.* Washington, D.C.: Federal Mediation and Conciliation Service, 1978.

Frank, J. D. *Sanity and Survival: Psychological Aspects of War and Peace.* New York: Random House, 1968.

Healy, J. J. (Ed.). *Creative Collective Bargaining.* Englewood Cliffs, N.J.: Prentice-Hall, 1965.

Popular, J. J., II. "Labor Management Relations by Objectives." In *Industrial Relations Guide.* Englewood Cliffs, N.J.: Prentice-Hall, 1977.

Thomas, K. W. "Conflict and Conflict Management." In M. D. Dunette (Ed.), *Handbook of Industrial and Organizational Psychology.* Chicago: Rand McNally, 1976.

Walton, R. E., and McKersie, R. B. *A Behavioral Theory of Labor Negotiations.* New York: McGraw Hill, 1965.

Robert Birnbaum, former chancellor of the University of Wisconsin at Oshkosh, is chairman of the Department of Higher and Adult Education at Teachers College, Columbia University. He first presented a version of this Chapter at the eighth annual conference of the National Center for the Study of Collective Bargaining in Higher Education, in April 1980.

*The acceptance of mediation and arbitration in labor disputes
has evolved gradually during the history of the United States.*

The Development of the Neutral Function in Labor Relations

James P. Begin

The purpose of this chapter is to review the emergence of the neutral function in the context of collective bargaining to determine whether or not it might have application to higher education impasses of the 1980s. That the use of the neutral function in labor relations is probably its most extensive and systematic application in society makes an analysis of it potentially profitable.

The story of the development of the neutral function in labor relations is essentially the story of the development and institutionalization of the collective bargaining process. The development of the collective bargaining process was, in turn, an adaptation made necessary by the growth of the industrial revolution's large and complex organizations. In the context of the organizational and environmental changes accompanying the industrial revolution, collective bargaining became an important mechanism for industrial democracy. The acceptance of the neutral process by the parties represented a recognition that while society was ready and willing to accept collective bargaining,

The author is appreciative of the background research done by Raymond G. Heineman, Jr., a graduate student in industrial relations and human resources at Rutgers University.

the impact of the collective bargaining process upon industrial organizations and society through strike activity had to be minimized. Thus over a period of several decades, the use of neutrals to resolve conflict has evolved into a permanent and important feature of the labor relations system.

Some of these threads can also be recognized in the higher education context and it is probable that many of the neutral tools can be adapted for usage to resolve organizational tensions in higher education.

Definitions

A number of terms have evolved over the years to describe the neutral tools used to resolve collective bargaining disputes. To begin, labor relations disputes can be divided into two types: *interest disputes* and *rights disputes.* Interest disputes involve disagreements arising out of the negotiations of a contract wherein the parties are "cutting up the pie," or, stated another way, allocating the resources of an organization, whether the resources involve money or authority. The completion of the negotiation process produces a contract which sets out the agreements of the parties in respect to resource allocation. In other words, the contract sets out the rights of the parties in respect to employee-employer issues. It follows, then, that disputes over the interpretation of applications of those agreements are rights disputes.

The terms used to describe the neutral functions that deal with interest and rights disputes are conciliation, mediation, fact finding with or without recommendations, voluntary arbitration, and compulsory arbitration. For the most part, these terms represent a continuum from the least amount of intervention in labor relations disputes by outside neutrals to the greatest.

The distinction between conciliation and mediation has become erased over the years with both processes now referring to the intervention of a third party who has no binding authority but rather serves as a catalyst to resolve the dispute. Conciliation is usually perceived as being a milder form of this type of intervention (Simkin, 1971). On the other end of the continuum is arbitration wherein the neutral has the binding authority to commit the parties. In voluntary arbitration, the parties mutually agree to accept the third party's binding decision; the experimental negotiating agreement in the U.S. Steelworkers' contract with the basic steel industry is an example. In compulsory arbitration the arbitration process is mandated by the government, usually by statute.

Fact finding with or without recommendations occupies the middle ground in respect to the authority of third-party neutrals. Presumably, the development of a systematic data base creates additional pressure on the parties to settle. Fact finding with recommendations is also equivalent to advisory arbitration where the parties do not have to accept the arbitrator's award.

In interest disputes, the most common tool used in the private sector is mediation. Arbitration of contract negotiation (interest) disputes is currently the exception in the private sector, with the steel industry agreement noted above as an example. In contrast, in the public sector, arbitration has been satisfactorily established in many states to resolve negotiations disputes, primarily for public safety bargaining units. The basis of the laws setting up interest arbitration is the absence of the right to strike in most states. Most states with public employees' bargaining laws also provide statutory two-step mediation and fact-finding procedures.

For contract interpretation (rights) disputes, the private sector has almost universally adopted binding arbitration as the quid pro quo for the forbearance from strikes over contract disputes during the term of the contract. The success of the procedure is illustrated by the fact that about 95 percent of the private sector contracts had incorporated this procedure by 1966 (U.S. Department of Labor, 1966). The use of binding contract arbitration in the public sector where collective bargaining is twenty years old is increasing as well, although many contracts still contain mediation, fact-finding, or advisory arbitration in the grievance process rather than binding arbitration. However, some states mandate binding contract arbitration because of the absence of the right to strike.

The Development of the Neutral Function in Labor Relations

The development of the dispute settlement terminology described above has been a twentieth-century phenomenon; in the nineteenth century these precise definitions had not yet evolved. Interestingly, the term arbitration referred not only to the mediation of contract negotiations disputes, but it also was used to describe the collective bargaining process. The term "collective bargaining" was not invented until after 1900 when the Webbs of England reportedly initiated its usage in their important bargaining publications (see Witte, 1952). Until the term collective bargaining developed, then, arbitration referred both to participation of third parties as well as the negotiations process. The state arbitration acts which were passed late in the nineteenth century, for example, were called arbitration acts, but what they really referred to was mediation as we know it today.

Collective action by employees emerged early in our nation's history, particularly amongst skilled trades such as cabinet makers, shoemakers, and printers. But the period prior to 1870 could be labeled the precollective bargaining era in this country since its dominant feature was the attempt of the courts to suppress the emerging pressures for collective action. From 1776, when the printers unionized in New York City, employee union activity developed slowly but in a very strong fashion (Schuck, 1976). With this emergence of collective action by employees came the development of neutral functions in the late nineteenth century.

The constitution of the cabinet makers in Philadelphia mentioned arbitration as early as 1829, but as has been stated above, arbitration at that time meant mediation as it is now defined. As industrialization progressed in the nineteenth century, spurred on particularly by the Civil War, so did the growth of the collective bargaining process. The late 1800s were marked by numerous, often bloody, confrontations between labor and management, one of the most notorious being the Homestead Massacre of 1892. This confrontation in the steel industry led to the loss of lives on both sides. It was this growth of collective bargaining, and the resulting battles, which provided the impetus to the development of neutral mechanisms (as noted by Witte, 1952, the first article about arbitration seems to have been published in 1871 by Eckley B. Coxe, describing the British arbitration boards, an indication that developments in this country were derived from earlier experiences in England).

When the government reacted to serious strikes by enacting arbitration laws in the late 1800s, arbitration still referred to mediation as it is currently defined. Reflecting the local market orientation of our economy at that time, public policy emerged only on the state level. Maryland was the first state to pass such a law in 1878, followed by laws in New Jersey, Pennsylvania, Ohio, Kansas, and finally Iowa in 1886 (Witte, 1952). Of the early laws, it appears that only the Pennsylvania law was ever utilized. The key point, however, is that it was the state governments which initiated the systematic development of neutral functions, as will be described below. The further institutionalization of these neutral functions into the collective bargaining process also relied heavily on government intervention.

The second generation of state laws in the nineteenth and early twentieth centuries were utilized to a greater extent, perhaps because the later state boards were comprised of full-time members. The earlier boards were often appointed on an ad hoc basis by the courts on the joint application of labor and management.

The federal government entered the picture with the passage of the Arbitration Act of 1888. This act was intended to deal with the labor-management disputes on railroads. However, the voluntary arbitration provisions were not used during the ten-year life of the Act. The low usage of this Act and the Erdman Act which replaced it in 1898 was due to the employers' refusal to use the provisions. It was this experience which led the American Federation of Labor to come out in opposition to compulsory arbitration in 1900 (Witte, 1952).

The state boards were not used much and they were often ineffective, but they were about all that was available in terms of third-party assistance, and they marked the beginning of modern dispute settlement. An indication of the growing acceptance of neutral functions in labor relations was the convening of the Congress on Industrial Conciliation and Arbitration in 1894. As with other developments in the history of mediation and arbitration, a strike (the Pullman strike) provided the impetus for this meeting.

After the turn of the century, the acceptance of neutral functions by employers increased as organizations such as the National Civic Federation promoted their usage. At its first conference in 1900 "the advantages of conciliation and arbitration were extolled by leaders of industry, labor, the church, and the general public" (Witte, 1952, pp. 17–18). At the same time the number of agreements between labor and management was increasing along with the growth of trade unionism. Many of these agreements provided for the mediation of interest disputes.

The first permanent procedures established for rights arbitration derived from a coal strike in 1902. A conciliation board was set up to settle disputes over the application of a settlement awarded by the Anthracite Coal Strike Commission established by the President to end the dispute. Strikes in the clothing industry and on the railways also provided the impetus for the development of neutral functions. In fact, prior to World War I, these were the only industries in which there were a sizable number of arbitration cases.

At the time of World War I, the collective bargaining movement was small but growing in employee acceptability. Additionally, arbitration (mediation) of strikes over negotiations of contracts had become generally acceptable. For example, the United States Conciliation Service was established within the Department of Labor in 1913. However, only labor experts as yet appreciated the distinction between "interest" and "rights" disputes. Arbitration dealing with contract interpretation and application matters dealt primarily with piece rate determination (Witte, 1952).

World War I has been described as marking a new era for the trade union movement in the United States. Union membership grew considerably and trade union leaders were given important roles in the resolution of labor strife during the war. The federal government, in an attempt to minimize the impact of strikes on the wartime economy, again played a major role in institutionalizing neutral functions. Labor leaders were provided memberships on the wartime boards and commissions set up by the government to deal with labor problems. The various boards were replaced by the National War Labor Board which functioned to 1919. The agency adjusted disputes through mediation by getting the parties to agree to arbitration or by outlining a basis for settlement. The Board rendered thirty-eight decisions of the latter variety which resembled arbitration awards since they were generally complied with, but after the Armistice the awards were not enforced and a period of tremendous strike activity began. This period produced the use of compulsory interest arbitration in the coal industry, the building trades in Chicago, the New York printing industry, and the clothing industry. The failure of these arbitrations destroyed the unions' faith in voluntary arbitration for some time.

At the same time, rights arbitration was taking hold, having received its start in the clothing industry before the war. Furthermore, rights arbitration had caught the fancy of academics who saw its evolution as the substitution of industrial law for chaos. Arbitration was further popularized by the rapid growth of commercial arbitration; the American Arbitration Association was founded in 1926 to deal with commercial disputes. Witte (1952) expressed the opinion that the most important development in the neutral field during the twenties was the move towards compulsory arbitration for interest disputes. However, the failure of these experiments on the state and federal levels further embittered the unions about this terminal procedure.

The onset of the depression and the resulting public policies supporting the collective bargaining process in the 1930s (for example, the Wagner Act passed in 1935) marked the beginning of the rapid growth of unionism and rights arbitration. Large manufacturing industries, which had held out against unionization, were organized one by one. With growth also occurring in smaller companies, new contracts were signed by the thousands and the growth of unionism continued during World War II.

The increase in the number of agreements explains the rapid growth of rights arbitration since the depression. "It was only in the 1930s that labor arbitration predominantly came to mean arbitration in grievance cases, and in the 1940s when this type of arbitration was experiencing its most rapid growth" (Witte, 1952, p. 49). An important impetus was the War Labor Board which encouraged the use of binding contract arbitration as a substitute for strikes over the interpretation or application of labor agreements. The National War Labor Board also served to provide a cadre of experienced arbitrators to provide needed arbitrators. In 1937, as well, the American Arbitration Association moved into the labor field and helped popularize arbitration of contract disputes. In 1947, the United States Conciliation Service was renamed the Federal Mediation and Conciliation Service. Many states also developed arbitration and mediation agencies. Clearly, dispute settlement in labor relations had come into its own after a rough beginning. In the period from 1900 to 1930, many states had abolished or abandoned nonfunctioning mediation and arbitration services (Witte, 1952). However, with the spread of unionism and strikes, state agencies once again emerged to play an active role in dispute resolution.

The greatest influence on postwar dispute resolution, particularly grievance arbitration, was the War Labor Board. Witte (1952, p. 58) described this effect as follows:

> Besides exercising functions during the War akin to, although not technically, arbitration, the National War Labor Board did a great deal to foster voluntary arbitration. Where labor-management agreements included a full grievance procedure for the settlement of disputes over the interpretation or application of contract provisions, the War Labor Board always insisted that this procedure be followed. Many cases were sent back to the parties where the labor agreement provided the means for final settlement. Where contracts lacked provisions for

the arbitration of such disputes as the final step in the grievance procedure, the War Labor Board often sent a case to arbitration, and in literally hundreds of disputes directed the insertion of complete grievance procedure, culminating in arbitration, in the labor-management agreements. To several large employers and their unions, the Board informally suggested the employment of permanent umpires to settle all unresolved disputes over the meaning of contracts.

At least equally important was the training the War Labor Board afforded to a great many people in the ranks of the public, labor, and industry, in the settlement of unresolved labor disputes. The great majority of the labor arbitrators of the present day gained their first direct experience in service on the staff of the War Labor Board or on its disputes panels. As has been noted, the War Labor Board and the following Labor-Management Conference undoubtedly were major factors accounting for the great spread of grievance arbitration in the 1940s.

Since World War II, the major developments in dispute resolution have been related to the emergence of public sector collective bargaining. Wisconsin enacted the first legislation permitting some public employees to unionize in 1959. When President Kennedy signed Executive Order 10988 in 1961 permitting federal employees to unionize, the door was opened. Many states enacted bargaining legislation within a few years. As noted previously, most statutes incorporated features of the dispute mechanisms developed in the private sector.

The adoption of the private sector dispute settlement models by the public sector indicates that in the collective bargaining context, these procedures were perceived to have provided a social good. Indeed, the success of the contract arbitration procedure prompted an academic to describe these procedures as one of society's greatest inventions.

Another development which brought arbitration back into the negotiating (interest) sphere was the signing of the Experimental Negotiating Agreement by the United States Steelworkers of America and ten basic steel companies. The agreement provided that if negotiations break down, a special panel of arbitrators is appointed. This agreement, unusual because unions in the private sector have strongly opposed interest arbitration, derives from the special economic condition of the steel industry. Foreign competition and substitute products have had a major effect on the health of the industry and thus on employment opportunities.

Additionally, the building up and working off of inventories in preparation for strikes also created layoffs and instability in the industry. These forces propelled the parties to seek more peaceful solutions. Other industrial bargaining units have failed to follow the steel industry's example, but the steel industry's apparent satisfaction so far is evidenced by the parties' renewal of the agreement for an additional three-year period.

Summary—Collective Bargaining

The institutionalization of dispute settlement mechanisms in collective bargaining evolved gradually over the decades to its current form and usage. The growth depended upon: (1) The economic, social, and organizational changes which were the consequence of the industrial revolution; (2) The growth and acceptance of collective bargaining as a means of decision making at the workplace; (3) A recognition that institutionalized conflict management was preferable to continuous work stoppages, particularly during war time; (4) An active role by government in encouraging the usage of dispute settlement procedures, first at the state level and then at the federal level as national markets developed. In short, collective bargaining and the related neutral mechanisms facilitated the adaptation of organizations to change by siphoning off tensions through the resolution of problems.

Relevance to Higher Education

At first consideration, the development of the neutral function in labor relations may not seem to be relevant for conflict resolution in higher education. The parties in conflict in industrial and manufacturing labor relations are seeking definite ends, either the negotiation of a contract or the resolution of a grievance, in a decision-making process which is protected by law. Here the neutral functions evolved to bring closure to the contract negotiations or interpretation processes in an effort to eliminate or minimize societal dislocations due to strikes. In higher education, however, except for employer-employee relations disputes where in many instances employees are already adapting to organizational stress through collective bargaining procedures, the same procedural context may not exist. For example, disputes between public and private institutions within a state over public resources or public control are not likely to lead to a strike or a boycott. Nor are the solutions likely to be embedded in an enforceable contract. On the other hand, student disputes may lead to strike-like behavior on the part of students, and it is possible that appropriate solutions to these types of disputes could be incorporated into agreements. Nonetheless, the use of third-party neutrals in both instances might be useful in improving communications, defusing tension, and resolving conflict short of costly and timely court proceedings.

One thing is certain: The changes expected over the next decade, as institutions of higher education adapt to major stress brought about by decreases in resources and enrollments, are certain to create opportunities where neutral intervention can be useful. The emergence of faculty bargaining over the past decade is one sign that organizational stress due to change is already upon us. The collective bargaining system not only is capable of providing trained neutrals to deal with nonemployee relations problems, but it stands as an example of how these neutrals have made a major societal contribution in adapting organizations to change. The decades of successful evolution of these tools should be proof to the higher education community that the tools should also be useful and acceptable for the resolutions of a broad range of disputes.

References

Aaron, B. "Employee Rights Under an Agreement: A Current Evaluation." *Monthly Labor Review,* 1971, *94* (8), 155.

Schuck, J. P. "The Evolution of Dispute Resolution and Prevention." Selected proceedings of 25th annual conference of the Association of Labor Mediation Agencies. Albany, N.Y.: Association of Labor Mediation Agencies, 1976.

Simkin, W. E. *Mediation and the Dynamics of Collective Bargaining.* Washington, D.C.: Bureau of National Affairs, 1971.

U.S. Department of Labor. *Major Collective Bargaining Agreements — Arbitration Proceedings.* Bureau of Labor Statistics Bulletin 1425 — 6. Washington, D.C.: U.S. Government Printing Office, 1966.

Witte, E. E. *Historical Survey of Labor Arbitration.* Philadelphia: University of Pennsylvania Press, 1952.

James P. Begin is professor of industrial relations and director, Institute of Management and Labor Relations at Rutgers University, where he has been a faculty member for eleven years. He has published widely in the area of public-sector collective bargaining, particularly in higher education.

A list of pertinent sources for further reference is provided.

Further Resources

Jane E. McCarthy

Readers who want to learn more about the theory of conflict, dispute resolution procedures, and mediation and negotiation strategy are directed to the following books and articles on these subjects.

Coser, L. *The Functions of Social Conflict.* New York: Macmillan, 1956.

Deutsch, M. *The Resolution of Conflict: Constructive and Destructive Processes.* New Haven, Conn.: Yale University Press, 1973.

Douglas, A. "The Peaceful Settlement of Industrial and Intergroup Disputes." *Journal of Conflict Resolution,* 1957, *1,* 69–81.

Druckman, D. (Ed.). *Negotiations: Social-Psychological Approaches to the Study of Negotiation.* Beverly Hills, Calif.: Sage, 1977.

Fleishman, E. A. "Leadership Climate, Human Relations Training, and Supervisory Behavior." *Personnel Psychology,* 1953, *6,* 205–222.

Hollander, E. P. *Leadership Dynamics: A Practical Guide to Effective Relationships.* New York: Free Press, 1978.

Homans, G. C. *Social Behavior: Its Elementary Forms.* (rev. ed.) New York: Harcourt, 1974.

Kressel, K. *Labor Mediation: An Exploratory Survey.* New York: Association of Labor Mediation Agencies, 1972.

Li, V. H. *Law Without Lawyers.* Stanford, Calif.: Stanford Alumni Association Press, 1977.

Lieberman, M. "Negotiations with Members of Your Own Team." *School Management,* 1971, *15,* 10–11.

Maple, F. F. *Shared Decision Making.* Beverly Hills, Calif.: Sage, 1977.

Nierenberg, G. I. *The Art of Negotiating.* New York: Cornerstone Library, 1968.

Riecken, H. W. "The Effect of Talkativeness on Ability to Influence Group Solutions to Problems." *Sociometry,* 1958, *21,* 309–321.

Rokeach, M. *The Open and Closed Mind.* New York: Basic Books, 1960.

Rubin, J. Z., and Brown, B. R. *The Social Psychology of Bargaining and Negotiation.* New York: Academic Press, 1975.

Schelling, T. C. *The Strategy of Conflict.* New York: Oxford University Press, 1963.

Simkin, W. *Mediation and the Dynamics of Collective Bargaining.* Washington, D.C.: Bureau of National Affairs, 1971.

Simon, H. A. *Administrative Behavior.* (3rd ed.) New York: Free Press, 1976.

Strauss, A. *Negotiations: Varieties, Contexts, Processes, and Social Order.* San Francisco: Jossey-Bass, 1978.

Swingle, P. (Ed.). *The Structure of Conflict.* New York: Academic Press, 1970.

Resource material directed to the discussion of disputes in higher education is extremely limited. For an overview of disputes and legal issues in higher education the following reference material is suggested reading.

Bok, D. C. "The Federal Government and the University." *The Public Interest,* 1980.

Breneman, D. W., and Finn, C. E., Jr. *Public Policy and Private Higher Education.* Washington, D.C.: The Brookings Institution, 1978.

15 Minute Report. "The Campus and the Courts." December 1979.

Finn, C. E., Jr. *Scholars, Dollars and Bureaucrats.* Washington, D.C.: The Brookings Institution, 1978.

Gouldner, H. "The Social Impact of Campus Litigation." *Ohio State University Journal of Higher Education,* 1980, *51,* (3, entire issue).

Hollander, P. A. *Legal Handbook for Educators.* Boulder, Colo.: Westview Press, 1978.

Mortimer, K. P., and Tierney, M. L. *The Three "R's" of the Eighties: Reduction, Reallocation, and Retrenchment.* Washington, D.C.: ERIC/AAHE, 1979.

Vago, S., and Marske, C. *Law as a Method of Conflict Resolution in Academia.* Unpublished paper, St. Louis University, November 1978.

Jane E. McCarthy is director of the Center for Mediation in Higher Education at the American Arbitration Association in New York.

Index

A

Aaron, B., 89
Accreditation: and jurisdictional dispute, 5; and mediation, 23–24
Administrators: mediation for, 19–31; new, and mediation, 22–23; professional reputation of, 21, 29; rights and responsibilities of, 20
American Arbitration Association, 86
American Association of Collegiate Registrars and Admissions Officers (AACRAO), 60
American Association of University Administrators (AAUA), vii, 62; background of, 19–21; concerns of, 21–24, 31; inquiry by, 24–25; mediators of, 27–28; procedures of, 24–27; reactions to, 28–30; review by, 26–27; users of, 27; visitation by, 25–26
American Association of University Professors (AAUP), vii, 45, 62; censure by, 13–14; Committee A on Academic Freedom and Tenure of, 10–13; history of, 9–10; informal mediation by, 14–16; investigation by, 13–14; scope of concerns by, 10–11; staff procedures of, 11–13
American Council on Education, 9, 45, 59, 66
American Federation of Labor, 84
Anthracite Coal Strike Commission, 85
Arbitration: development of, 81–98; mediation, distinct from, 3; as term, 83; uses of, 83
Arbitration Act of 1888, 84
Association of American Colleges, 9
Association of Governing Boards of Univesities and Colleges, 9, 45

B

Begin, J. P., viii, 81–89
Birnbaum, R., viii, 69–79
Blake, R. R., 76, 78
Bok, D. C., 58, 67, 92
Boston University, manuscript litigation of, 4

Breneman, D. W., 92
Brown, B. R., 92
Brown University, sex-discrimination suit at, vii
Buckley Amendment, 44

C

Canada, and AAUA, 19
Canadian Association of University Teachers, 14
Caplan, A. L., 59n, 67
Carnegie Commission on Higher Education, 45
Carnegie Council on Policy Studies in Higher Education, 45, 48
Censure, by AAUP, 13–14
Center for Mediation in Higher Education, vii, 2, 4, 7–8, 62–63
China, conflict resolution in, 50
Civil Rights Act of 1964, Title VI of, 44
Clark, T. B., 67
Collective bargaining: academic, 69–79; competition, compromise, and colaboration in, 70–72; continuous, 75; definitions in, 82–83; generalizations on, 71–72; neutral function in, 81–89; new approaches to, 74–77; potential for, 77–78; problem solving focus in, 75; problems of, 72–74; structure changed for, 76–77; third parties used in, 75–76
Collegiality, and mediation, 4
Conciliation, mediation related to, 82
Confidentiality, issue of, 36
Conflict: areas of, 2–3, 21–24, 37–41; attitudes toward, 1, 51; constructive, in bargaining, 69–79; destructive, 69; financially related, 2, 22, 37; with governing board, 33–42; and mediation in higher education, 1–8; off- and on-campus, 2; presence of, 1; resources on, 91–92; role of, 1
Congress on Industrial Conciliation and Arbitration, 84
Consultation, rather than mediation, 36

Consumer Product Safety Commission, 57–58

Coser, L., 91

Court cases, and grievance procedures, 44

Coxe, E. B., 84

D

Davis, B. H., 17

d'Errico, P., vii, 49–54

Deutsch, M., 69, 76, 78–79, 91

Dewey, J., 9–10, 17

Dismissal for cause, and mediation, 15

Dispute Resolution Center, 52–54, 65

Douglas, A., 91

Druckman, D., 72, 79, 91

E

Education Amendments of 1972, Title IX of, 44

Edwards, H. T., 43, 48, 67

El-Khawas, E., 48

Employment, written conditions of, and mediation, 21–22

Environmental Protection Agency, 57

Equal Employment Opportunity Commission (EEOC), 61, 63

Erdman Act of 1898, 84

Evergreen State College, and veterans' benefits, 59

Executive Order 10988, 87

Executive Order 11246, 44

F

Fact finding, 82

Family Educational Rights and Privacy Act of 1974, 44

Federal Mediation and Conciliation Service (FMCS), 78, 79, 86

Federal Trade Commission, 57

Financial conflicts, 2, 22, 37

Finn, C. E., Jr., 56–57, 67, 92

Fleishman, E. A., 91

Folger, J., vii, 43–48

Food and Drug Administration, 57

Frank, J. D., 72, 79

Freedman, J. O., 65, 68

G

Gouldner, H., 92

Governance structures, and mediation, 23

Governing boards: actions of, and mediation, 22; and confidence, 39–41; conflicts with, 33–42; divided, 28; domination of, 38–39; and mediation potential, 34–37; president's relationship with, 33–34; self-perceptions of, 35; and situations needing mediation, 37–41; and special interests, 39

Government regulations: alternatives to, 55–68; and avoiding grievances, 60–64; and expert tribunals, 66; future procedures, 44; and mediation, 24, 62–63; methods of, 57–58; origins and trends of, 56–58; role of, 55–56; and self-regulation, 57–60, 67

Grievance procedures: avoiding need for, 60–64; functions and implications of, 47–48; future for, 66; history of, 43–45; and mediation, 8, 64–65; for students, 43–48

H

Healy, J. J., 74, 78, 79

Heineman, R. G., Jr., 81n

Herman, S., 65, 68

Higher Education: conflict and mediation in, 1–8; resources on disputes in, 92

Hollander, E. P., 91

Hollander, P. A., vii, 19–31, 92

Homans, G. C., 91

Homestead Massacre, 84

I

Incompatibility, and mediation, 22

Interest disputes, 82

Internal remedies, exhaustion of, 29, 30

Iowa, labor laws in, 84

K

Kansas, labor laws in, 84

Katsh, E., vii, 49–54

Kaysen, C., 63–64, 68

Kennedy, J. F., 87

Kressel, K., 91

Kurland, J. E., vii, 9–17

L

Law, legal studies distinct from, 49–50

Legal studies: courses in, 49–51; and mediation, 49–54

Li, V. H., 91
Lieberman, M., 91
Litigation, limitations of, 51
Lloyd-Campbell, C. C., 61, 68

M

McCarthy, J. E., vii–viii, 1–8, 91–92
McKersie, R. B., 77, 79
MacVittie, R. W., 20n
Maple, F. F., 92
Marske, C., 92
Maryland, labor laws in, 84
Massachusetts, University of, at Amherst, Legal Studies Program at, vii–viii, 50–54, 65
Massachusetts Institute of Technology, mediation and ombudsman service at, 64–65, 66
Mediation: of AAUA standards, 19–31; of AAUP standards, 9–17; for administrators, 19–31; arbitration distinct from, 3; barriers to, 5–6; counciliation related to, 82; and conflict in higher education, 1–8; and costs, 8, 28; development of, 81–89; effective, 6–7; future of, 31, 66; and government regulations, 24, 62–63; and grievance procedures, 8, 64–65, informality of, 6, 14–16; and legal studies, 49–54; as maintenance, 41; potential for, 4–5, 34–37; process of, 3–4; reactions to, 28–30; written agreements unnecessary in, 6–7, 27
Mediators: selection of, 27–28; tasks of, 3–4
Medical disability, and mediation, 16
Michigan, University of, Rackham School of Graduate Studies at, vii, 45–48
Mortimer, K. P., 92
Mouton, J. S., 76, 78

N

National Civic Federation, 85
National War Labor Board, 85, 86–87
Neutral functions: analysis of, 81–89; in higher education, 88–89; historical development of, 83–88
New Jersey, labor laws in, 84
Nierenberg, G. I., 92
Nordby, V., 46–47, 48

Nordin, V. D., 43, 48
Northeastern University, grievance procedure at, 65

O

Occupational Safety and Health Administration, 57
Office of Civil Rights, 63
Ohio, labor laws in, 84

P

Peltason, J., 58–59, 68
Pennsylvania, labor laws in, 84
Pennsylvania, University of, ombudsman at, 65–66
Phi Beta Kappa, 14
Pool, I. D. S., 59n, 68
Popular, J. J., II, 78, 79
Power and authority, and mediation, 36–37
President: confidence in, 39–41; governing board relationship with, 33–34
Pride of position, and mediation, 34–35
Private institutions: and finance dilemma, 37; and state board guidelines, 5
Probation and tenure, mediation for, 15–16
Public institutions, and finance dilemmas, 37

R

Rehabilitation Act of 1973, Section 504 of, 44
Research, with human subjects, and self-regulation, 59
Riecken, H. W., 92
Rifkin, J., vii, 49–54
Rights disputes, 82
Rokeach, M., 92
Rowe, M. P., 64–65, 68
Rubin, J. Z., 92
Rutgers, manuscript litigation of, 4

S

Schelling, T. C., 92
Schuck, J. P., 82, 89
Seabury, P., 60, 68
Self-regulation, and government regulation, 57–60, 67

Shubert, J., vii, 43–48
Simkin, W. E., 82, 89, 92
Simon, H. A., 92
Singer, L., 63, 68
Sloma, R. L., 76, 78
Social Security Administration, 60
Stamato, L., viii, 55–68
Stark, J., 45, 48
State boards, disputes with, 5
State University of New York, Buffalo, 19
Statler, S., 58, 68
Strauss, A., 92
Students, grievance procedures for, 43–48
Swingle, P., 92

T

Termination: and mediation, 21–24; notice of, 16
Thomas, K. W., 70, 79
Tierney, M. L., 92

U

United Kingdom: and AAUA, 19; arbitration in, 83, 84; censure listing in, 14
United States Conciliation Service, 85, 86

U.S. Department of Health and Human Services, 59
U.S. Department of Health, Education, and Welfare, 63
U.S. Department of Labor, 83, 85, 89
U.S. Steelworkers of America, 82, 87
Urban Court Mediation Project, 53

V

Vago, S., 92
Veterans Administration, 59–60

W

Wagner Act of 1935, 86
Walton, R. E., 77, 79
Wayne State University, and veterans' benefits, 59
Webb, B. P., 83
Webb, S. J., 83
Wilson College, closing decision for, 4–5
Wisconsin, labor laws in, 87
Witte, E. E., 83, 84, 85, 86–87, 89

Z

Zwingle, J. L., vii, 33–42

New Directions Quarterly Sourcebooks

New Directions for Higher Education is one of several distinct series of quarterly sourcebooks published by Jossey-Bass. The sourcebooks in each series are designed to serve both as *convenient compendiums* of the latest knowledge and practical experience on their topics and as *long-life reference tools.*

One-year, four-sourcebook subscriptions for each series cost $18 for individuals (when paid by personal check) and $30 for institutions, libraries, and agencies. Single copies of earlier sourcebooks are available at $6.95 each *prepaid* (or $7.95 each when *billed*).

A complete listing is given below of current and past sourcebooks in the *New Directions for Higher Education* series. The titles and editors-in-chief of the other series are also listed. To subscribe, or to receive further information, write: New Directions Subscriptions, Jossey-Bass Inc., Publishers, 433 California Street, San Francisco, California 94104.

New Directions for Higher Education
JB Lon Hefferlin, Editor-in-Chief
1973: 1. *Facilitating Faculty Development,* Mervin Freedman
   2. *Strategies for Budgeting,* George Kaludis
   3. *Services for Students,* Joseph Katz
   4. *Evaluating Learning and Teaching,* Robert Pace
1974: 5. *Encountering the Unionized University,* Jack Schuster
   6. *Implementing Field Experience Education,* Jack Duley
   7. *Avoiding Conflict in Faculty Personnel Practices,* Richard Peairs
   8. *Improving Statewide Planning,* James Wattenbarger, Louis Bender
1975: 9. *Planning the Future of the Undergraduate College,* Donald Trites
  10. *Individualizing Education by Learning Contracts,* Neal Berte
  11. *Meeting Women's New Educational Needs,* Clare Rose
  12. *Strategies for Significant Survival,* Clifford Stewart, Thomas Harvey
1976: 13. *Promoting Consumer Protection for Students,* Joan Stark
  14. *Expanding Recurrent and Nonformal Education,* David Harman
  15. *A Comprehensive Approach to Institutional Development,* William Bergquist, William Shoemaker
  16. *Improving Educational Outcomes,* Oscar Lenning

1977: 17. *Renewing and Evaluating Teaching,* John Centra
18. *Redefining Service, Research, and Teaching,*
    Warren Martin
19. *Managing Turbulence and Change,* John Millett
20. *Increasing Basic Skills by Developmental Studies,*
    John Roueche
1978: 21. *Marketing Higher Education,* David W. Barton, Jr.
22. *Developing and Evaluating Administrative Leadership,*
    Charles F. Fisher
23. *Admitting and Assisting Students after Bakke,*
    Alexander W. Astin, Bruce Fuller, Kenneth C. Green
24. *Institutional Renewal Through the Improvement of
    Teaching,* Jerry G. Gaff
1979: 25. *Assuring Access for the Handicapped,* Martha Ross Redden
26. *Assessing Financial Health,* Carol Frances,
    Sharon L. Coldren
27. *Building Bridges to the Public,* Louis T. Benezet,
    Frances W. Magnusson
28. *Preparing for the New Decade,* Larry W. Jones,
    Franz A. Nowotny
1980: 29. *Educating Learners of All Ages,* Elinor Greenberg,
    Kathleen M. O'Donnell, William Bergquist
30. *Managing Facilities More Effectively,* Harvey H. Kaiser
31. *Rethinking College Responsibilities for Values,*
    Mary Louise McBee

New Directions for Child Development
William Damon, Editor-in-Chief

New Directions for College Learning Assistance
Kurt V. Lauridsen, Editor-in-Chief

New Directions for Community Colleges
Arthur M. Cohen, Editor-in-Chief
Florence B. Brawer, Associate Editor

New Directions for Continuing Education
Alan B. Knox, Editor-in-Chief

New Directions for Exceptional Children
James J. Gallagher, Editor-in-Chief

New Directions for Experiential Learning
Pamela J. Tate, Editor-in-Chief
Morris T. Keeton, Consulting Editor

New Directions for Institutional Advancement
A. Westley Rowland, Editor-in-Chief

New Directions for Institutional Research
Marvin W. Peterson, Editor-in-Chief

New Directions for Mental Health Services
H. Richard Lamb, Editor-in-Chief

New Directions for Methodology of Social and Behavioral Science
Donald W. Fiske, Editor-in-Chief

New Directions for Program Evaluation
Scarvia B. Anderson, Editor-in-Chief

New Directions for Student Services
Ursula Delworth and Gary R. Hanson, Editors-in-Chief

New Directions for Teaching and Learning
Kenneth E. Eble and John Noonan, Editors-in-Chief

New Directions for Testing and Measurement
William B. Schrader, Editor-in-Chief

STATEMENT OF OWNERSHIP, MANAGEMENT, AND CIRCULATION
(Required by 39 U.S.C. 3685)

1. Title of Publication: New Directions for Higher Education. A. Publication number: USPS 990-880. 2. Date of filing: September 29, 1980. 3. Frequency of issue: quarterly. A. Number of issues published annually: four. B. Annual subscription price: $30 institutions; $18 individuals. 4. Location of known office of publication: 433 California Street, San Francisco (San Francisco County), California 94104. 5. Location of the headquarters or general business offices of the publishers: 433 California Street, San Francisco (San Francisco County), California 94104. 6. Names and addresses of publisher, editor, and managing editor: publisher—Jossey-Bass Inc., Publishers, 433 California Street, San Francisco, California 94104; editor—JB Lon Hefferlin, 433 California Street, San Francisco, CA 94104; managing editor—JB Lon Hefferlin, 433 California Street, San Francisco, California 94104. 7. Owner: Jossey-Bass Inc., Publishers, 433 California Street, San Francisco, California 94104. 8. Known bondholders, mortgages, and other security holders owning or holding 1 percent or more of total amount of bonds, mortgages, or other securities: same as No. 7. 10. Extent and nature of circulation: (Note: first number indicates the average number of copies of each issue during the preceding twelve months; the second number indicates the actual number of copies published nearest to filing date.) A. Total number of copies printed (net press run): 2552, 2555. B. Paid circulation, 1) Sales through dealers and carriers, street vendors, and counter sales: 110, 140. 2) Mail subscriptions: 1299, 998. C. Total paid circulation: 1409, 1138. D. Free distribution by mail, carrier, or other means (samples, complimentary, and other free copies): 125, 125. E. Total distribution (sum of C and D): 1534, 1263. F. Copies not distributed, 1) Office use, left over, unaccounted, spoiled after printing: 1018, 1292. 2) Returns from news agents: 0, 0. G. Total (sum of E, F1, and 2—should equal net press run shown in A): 2552, 2555.

I certify that the statements made by me above are correct and complete.

JOHN R. WARD
Vice-President